EDUCATING TEACHERS
of Science, Mathematics, and Technology
—— New Practices for the New Millennium ——

Committee on Science and Mathematics Teacher Preparation

Center for Education
National Research Council

NATIONAL ACADEMY PRESS
Washington, DC

NATIONAL ACADEMY PRESS   2101 Constitution Avenue, N.W.   Washington, D.C. 20418

NOTICE: The project that is the subject of this report was approved by the Governing Board of the National Research Council, whose members are drawn from the councils of the National Academy of Sciences, the National Academy of Engineering, and the Institute of Medicine. The members of the committee responsible for the report were chosen for their special competences and with regard for appropriate balance.

This study was supported by Contract/Grant No. DUE 9614007 between the National Academy of Sciences and the National Science Foundation. Any opinions, findings, conclusions, or recommendations expressed in this publication are those of the author(s) and do not necessarily reflect the views of the organizations or agencies that provided support for the project.

Library of Congress Cataloging-in-Publication Data

Educating teachers of science, mathematics, and technology : new
practices for the new millennium / Committee on Science and Mathematics
        p. cm.
Includes bibliographical references and index.
  ISBN 0-309-07033-3
1. Science teachers—Training of—United States. 2. Mathematics
teachers—Training of—United States. 3. Engineering teachers—Training
of—United States. I. National Research Council (U.S.). Committee on
Science and Mathematics Teacher Preparation. II. Title.
  Q183.3.A1 E39 2000
  507'.1'073—dc21
                                00-011135

Additional copies of this report are available from the National Academy Press, 2101 Constitution Avenue, N.W., Lockbox 285, Washington, D.C. 20055; (800) 624-6242 or (202) 334-3313 (in the Washington metropolitan area); Internet, http://www.nap.edu

Printed in the United States of America

First Printing, January 2000
Second Printing, April 2002

THE NATIONAL ACADEMIES

National Academy of Sciences
National Academy of Engineering
Institute of Medicine
National Research Council

The *National Academy of Sciences* is a private, nonprofit, self-perpetuating society of distinguished scholars engaged in scientific and engineering research, dedicated to the furtherance of science and technology and to their use for the general welfare. Upon the authority of the charter granted to it by the Congress in 1863, the Academy has a mandate that requires it to advise the federal government on scientific and technical matters. Dr. Bruce M. Alberts is president of the National Academy of Sciences.

The *National Academy of Engineering* was established in 1964, under the charter of the National Academy of Sciences, as a parallel organization of outstanding engineers. It is autonomous in its administration and in the selection of its members, sharing with the National Academy of Sciences the responsibility for advising the federal government. The National Academy of Engineering also sponsors engineering programs aimed at meeting national needs, encourages education and research, and recognizes the superior achievements of engineers. Dr. William A. Wulf is president of the National Academy of Engineering.

The *Institute of Medicine* was established in 1970 by the National Academy of Sciences to secure the services of eminent members of appropriate professions in the examination of policy matters pertaining to the health of the public. The Institute acts under the responsibility given to the National Academy of Sciences by its congressional charter to be an adviser to the federal government and, upon its own initiative, to identify issues of medical care, research, and education. Dr. Kenneth I. Shine is president of the Institute of Medicine.

The *National Research Council* was organized by the National Academy of Sciences in 1916 to associate the broad community of science and technology with the Academy's purposes of furthering knowledge and advising the federal government. Functioning in accordance with general policies determined by the Academy, the Council has become the principal operating agency of both the National Academy of Sciences and the National Academy of Engineering in providing services to the government, the public, and the scientific and engineering communities. The Council is administered jointly by both Academies and the Institute of Medicine. Dr. Bruce M. Alberts and Dr. William A. Wulf are chairman and vice chairman, respectively, of the National Research Council.

NATIONAL RESEARCH COUNCIL STAFF

JAY B. LABOV, Study Director (since October 1998)
JANE O. SWAFFORD, Senior Program Officer (January – October 1999)
NANCY L. DEVINO, Senior Program Officer (through October 1998)
TERRY K. HOLMER, Senior Project Assistant

Consultants

PAUL J. KUERBIS, Special Consultant, Colorado College
KATHLEEN (KIT) S. JOHNSTON, Consulting Editor

Reviewers

This report has been reviewed in draft form by individuals chosen for their diverse perspectives and technical expertise, in accordance with procedures approved by the National Research Council's Report Review Committee. The purpose of this independent review is to provide candid and critical comments that will assist the institution in making the published report as sound as possible and to ensure that the report meets institutional standards for objectivity, evidence, and responsiveness to the study charge. The review comments and draft manuscript remain confidential to protect the integrity of the deliberative process. We wish to thank the following individuals for their participation in the review of this report:

DAVID C. BERLINER, Arizona State University
FRANK CARDULLA, Lake Forest High School, Lake Forest, IL
JERE CONFREY, University of Texas at Austin
SARAH C. ELGIN, Washington University, St. Louis, MO
HENRY HEIKKINEN, University of Northern Colorado
TOBY M. HORN, Virginia Polytechnic Institute and State University
WILLIAM G. HOWARD, JR.*, Independent Consultant, Scottsdale, AZ
RONALD L. LATANISION***,** Massachusetts Institute of Technology
CHRISTINE WEST PATERACKI, Cario Middle School, Mt. Pleasant, SC
JUDITH ROITMAN, University of Kansas
THOMAS ROMBERG, University of Wisconsin, Madison
JAMES STITH, American Institute of Physics, College Park, MD

While the individuals listed above have provided many constructive comments and suggestions, responsibility for the final content of this report rests solely with the authoring committee and the National Research Council.

---

*Member of the National Academy of Engineering

Foreword

The United States is finally getting serious about the quality of our children's education, and it is rare to pick up a newspaper today without finding some discussion of education issues. In the current maelstrom of the education debate, the need to improve the quality of our teachers' preparation and professional development deserves a central place. Teachers stand at the center of any education system, since everything rests on their skills and energy. Questions regarding teaching quality, teaching effectiveness, and teacher recruitment and retention have become particularly important in science and mathematics, as we enter a century that will be ever more dependent on science and technology.

Many interacting and often-conflicting variables have influenced attempts to improve teaching in science and mathematics. These include a multitude of reports and recommendations from commissions and professional organizations; the increasing use of high-stakes standardized testing to measure the academic performance of students, teachers, and schools; and the reality of the many challenges that teachers and students actually face in today's classrooms.

The entire nation must recognize that teaching is a very difficult and demanding profession. Teachers must of course have a deep understanding of their subject areas, but this is not enough. They must also be skilled at motivating their students to want to learn in a society in which young people are exposed to so many outside distractions. Most importantly, improvements in teacher education need to be aligned with recommendations about what students should know and be able to do at various grade levels, which means that teachers need to become expert at what is called content-oriented pedagogy.

The National Academies recently called for a decade of research to be devoted to improving education (National Research Council, 1999c). A primary focus of that effort will be devoted to resolving issues about the most effective ways to improve teaching. It is in this context that the Academies also established the Committee on Science and Mathematics Teacher Preparation. If the nation is to make the continuous improvements needed in teaching, we need to make a science out of teacher education—using evidence and analysis to build an effective system of teacher preparation and professional development. What do we know about what works based on experience and research?

After two years of studying and synthesizing the immense body of research data—as well as recommendations from professional organizations and the diversity of current practices—the committee has issued this report. *Educating Teachers of Science, Mathematics, and Technology: New Practices for the New Millennium* will help readers understand areas of emerging consensus about what constitutes effective structure and practice for teacher education in these subject areas. The extensive list of cited references, many from peer-reviewed journals, reflect the committee's efforts to produce a report that will advance the scholarship of teacher education.

The report does more than review current data and issues. Importantly, it also offers a series of recommendations, based on extensive evidence from research, about how various stakeholders might contribute individually and collectively—even systemically—to the improvement of teaching in these subject areas. A number of critical points are emphasized:

1. Teacher education must no longer be viewed as a set of disconnected phases for which different communities assume the primary responsibility. As this study progressed, committee members realized that the committee's name (Committee on Science and Mathematics Teacher Preparation) was too limiting, because "preparation" is only one phase of "teacher education." Teacher education should instead be a seamless continuum that begins well before prospective teachers enter college and that supports them throughout their professional careers. Accordingly, this report calls for school districts, institutions of higher education (both two- and four-year colleges and universities), business, industry, research facilities, and individual scientists and other members of the community to work closely together in integrated, collaborative partnerships to support teachers and teacher education.

2. Responsibility for teacher education in science, mathematics, and technology can no longer be delegated only to schools of education and school districts. Scientists, mathematicians, and engineers must become more informed about and involved with this effort. Those who commit part of their professional lives to improving teacher education must be recognized and rewarded for their efforts. Moreover, since prospective teachers of science, mathematics, and technology are sitting in most college classrooms, all faculty who teach undergraduates in these subject areas need to think about how their courses can better meet the needs of these critical individuals. The committee has emphasized that changing courses in ways that address the needs of prospective and practicing teachers would also enhance the educational experience for most undergraduates.

3. If teaching is to improve, then teachers must be accorded the same kind of respect that members of other professions receive. As in other professions, beginning teachers cannot be expected to have mastered all that they will need to know and be able to do when they first begin teaching. Rather, the committee calls for a new emphasis on ongoing professional development that enables teachers to grow in their profession and to assume new responsibilities for their colleagues, their employers, and for future generations of teachers.

4. The ultimate measure of the success of any teacher education program is how well the students of these teachers learn and achieve. Thus, the partnerships that the committee envisions in this report would be structured in ways that facilitate student learning and the assessment of that learning.

Improving the quality of science and mathematics teaching, the professionalism of teaching, and the incentives and rewards in teaching are issues that are now deemed to be critical to the national interest. For this reason, in 1999 U.S. Secretary of Education Richard Riley established the National Commission on Mathematics and Science Teaching in the 21st Century, chaired by former Senator John Glenn of Ohio. In the same spirit, *Educating Teachers of Science, Mathematics, and Technology: New Practices for the New Millennium* is being made freely available on the Worldwide Web, so as to offer its valuable information and insights to as broad an audience as possible.

Bruce Alberts, President
National Academy of Sciences

Preface

In 1998, the National Research Council (NRC) established the Committee on Science and Mathematics Teacher Preparation (CSMTP) and charged it with identifying critical issues in existing practices and policies for K-12 teacher preparation in science and mathematics. In its Statement of Task, the NRC's Governing Board also asked the committee to identify recommendations from professional organizations regarding teacher preparation and the quality of the K-12 teaching of science and mathematics and to examine relevant research. The committee's report was to synthesize critical issues, recommendations, and relevant research.

In carrying out its responsibilities, the committee explored practices and policies in K-12 teacher education in general—for both prospective and currently practicing teachers—then focused on issues involving the teaching of science, mathematics, and technology.

Members examined the relevant literature and current calls for reform of K-16 science and mathematics education as well as more general principles of effective teacher education that can be derived from analysis of actual classroom practice. Research on what is currently known about effective teacher preparation and professional development and the committee's reflections on the compelling evidence for teacher education to become a career-long continuum lie at the foundation of the committee's discussion, conclusions, and subsequent vision and recommendations.

In reflecting on the committee's findings, members developed six principles to frame their conclusions about the need for changes in the predominant ways K-12 teachers of science, mathematics, and technology are currently prepared and professionally supported. The principles call for teacher education and teaching in science, mathematics, and technology improvement to be viewed as a top national priority; for the education of teachers to become a career-long process—a continuum—that stimulates teachers' intellectual growth as well as upgrades their knowledge and skills; for teaching as a profession to be upgraded in status and stature; for two- and four-year colleges and universities to assume greater responsibility and be held more accountable for improving teacher education; for institutions of higher education and K-12 schools to work together—along with the larger community—to improve teacher education; and for more scientists, mathematicians, and engineers to provide teachers with the appropriate content knowledge and pedagogy of their disciplines.

The report then describes how teacher preparation might be redesigned in light of research and new knowledge about how teachers learn the content, the art, and craft of their profession. The report also examines and provides examples of exemplary and promising current practices for improving teacher education, including establishment of close local or regional partnerships between school districts and teacher educators, scientists, and mathematicians in institutions of higher education. As they exist on a small scale today, these partnerships are devoted to improving student learning through improving the education and professional support of teachers.

After exploring what is known about the effectiveness of such collaborative approaches, the committee calls in its vision and specific recommendations for a fundamental rethinking and restructuring of the ways that the K-12 and higher education communities work toward improving teacher education, from initial preparation through life-long professional development.

To assist action on these principles, the committee calls in its recommendations for K-12 schools and districts and the higher education community—with support and assistance from the broader community—to engage in collaborative partnerships. In these partnerships, school districts and their higher education partners together would promote high-quality teacher education, including sharing responsibility for teacher preparation and on-going professional development for the K-12 partner schools' teachers.[1]

---

[1]The committee emphasizes in this report that all colleges and universities, including those that do not have formal teacher education programs, should become more involved with improving teacher education because the nation's teacher workforce consists of many individuals who have matriculated at all types of two- and four-year institutions of higher education. Although many of these schools do not offer formal teacher education programs, virtually every institution of higher education, through the kinds of courses it offers, the teaching it models, and the advising it provides to students, has the potential to influence whether or not its graduates will pursue careers in teaching.

Such partnerships will require a fundamental rethinking of the currently disparate phases of teacher education and, therefore, a fundamental restructuring of current organizational *and financial* relationships between the K-12 and higher education communities in science, mathematics, engineering, and technology (SME&T). Committee members readily acknowledge that this will not be a straightforward, easily accomplished, or inexpensive process. In these new partnerships, responsibility for preparatory student teaching experiences would be vested primarily in school district partners. In turn, responsibility for ongoing professional development would fall primarily within the purview of the higher education partners. These changes will require a tremendous shift in the structure, allocation of support resources, and relationships between the K-12 and higher education communities. And the result will be nothing less than the fundamental revamping of teaching as a profession.

The report before you addresses a broad audience because it is evident from the research that anyone who is responsible for any aspect of teacher preparation in science, mathematics, and technology education can no longer work in isolation if they are to help improve teacher education. All professional stakeholders in teacher education are addressed. They include teachers of science, mathematics, and technology, those in policy making institutions, accrediting agencies, and professional societies, as well as scientists, mathematicians, educators, and administrators inside and outside of academe.

The committee is confident that the report will prove useful to the many dedicated people who are working to improve the quality of the education of teachers of K-12 science, mathematics, and technology. The report also should help increase the numbers of teachers who are teaching in ways that allow their students to understand and appreciate science, mathematics, and technology and the relevance of these disciplines to virtually every aspect of our lives in the new millennium.

Herbert K. Brunkhorst
W.J. (Jim) Lewis
Co-Chairs
Committee on Science and
Mathematics Teacher Preparation

Dedication

Just prior to the publication of this report, we learned of the untimely and tragic death of Dr. Susan Loucks-Horsley. From 1998 until 1999, Susan was Director of K-12 Professional Development and Outreach in the National Research Council's Center for Science, Mathematics, and Engineering Education. Dr. Loucks-Horsley's work in professional development for teachers and the continual improvement of education for children was associated with many national organizations throughout her remarkable thirty-year career. One of Susan's proudest personal achievements, for which she was senior author, was the publication in 1998 of *Designing Professional Development for Teachers of Science and Mathematics*. Earlier, she led the development team of Facilitating Systemic Change in Science and Mathematics Education: A Toolkit for Professional Developers, the product of ten regional education laboratories. She also was on the development team of the Concerns-Based Adoption Model, which described how individuals experience change. At the time of her death, Susan was Associate Executive Director of the Biological Sciences Curriculum Study in Colorado Springs.

With this report and other publications that will surely follow on the importance of providing quality professional development for teachers, Susan's legacy of groundbreaking research, published works, and professional development and leadership initiatives for science education will continue. As some of her work is cited in this report, and she was a colleague, friend, and mentor to many on our committee and staff, we dedicate this report to Susan Loucks-Horsley. She will be greatly missed.

Acknowledgments

The members and staff of the Committee on Science and Mathematics Teacher Preparation are grateful to many people for their professional input and perspective to this study. We acknowledge the following people for providing presentations, additional data, and their invaluable insight and expertise to the committee during committee meetings:

Ismat Abdal-Haqq, American Association of Colleges for Teacher Education

Angelo Collins, Interstate New Teacher Assessment and Support Consortium

Linda Darling-Hammond, National Commission on Teaching and America's Future, and Stanford University

Emily Feistritzer, National Center for Education Information

Glenn F. Nyre, Westat

Abigail Smith, Teach for America

Jan Somerville, Education Trust

William Thompson, Interstate New Teacher Assessment and Support Consortium

Terry Woodin, Program Officer, Division of Undergraduate Education, National Science Foundation

Judith Wurtzel, Learning First Alliance

We also acknowledge and thank several colleagues from the National Research Council for their guidance and support:

Rodger Bybee, now Director of the Biological Sciences Curriculum Study, served as Executive Director of the National Research Council's Center for Science, Mathematics, and Engineering Education from the time that this project was conceived through June 1999. Rodger's contributions to this study are numerous, especially in helping the committee to set its priorities and in guiding the committee's staff for much of the study.

Joan Ferrini-Mundy, now Associate Dean for the Division of Science and Mathematics Education at Michigan State University, served as Associate

Executive Director of the National Research Council's Center for Science, Mathematics, and Engineering Education from the time that this project was conceived through June 1999. Joan's knowledge and insights about mathematics education, her understanding of the critical role of quality teacher education in promoting learning and academic achievement for all students, and her advice for completing this study are especially appreciated.

Eugenia Grohman, Kirsten Sampson Snyder, and **Yvonne Wise** were responsible for helping to shepherd the committee's report through the National Research Council's report review process. They assisted with recruiting reviewers, maintaining communication between the committee and the review monitor and coordinator during the response to review process, and working with National Academy Press and the National Academies' Office of News and Public Information.

Tina Winters worked with the committee's staff during a portion of 1998 in searching the literature on teacher education issues.

To all of these people, we express our gratitude and thanks.

Contents

EDUCATING TEACHERS
of Science, Mathematics, and Technology

Executive Summary

CURRENT PROBLEMS AND ISSUES IN TEACHER EDUCATION AND THE TEACHING PROFESSION

A large and growing body of research data—as well as recommendations from professional societies—indicate that the preparation and ongoing professional development of teachers in science, mathematics, and technology[1] for grades K-12 needs rethinking and improvement, and not just on a small scale. There is now a great deal of evidence that this situation permeates much of the system of teacher preparation and professional development, including the recruiting, preparing, inducting, and retaining of teachers. Indeed, many teachers themselves report frustration with current methods of and approaches to teacher education.

After extensive review of the research literature and the recommendations of professional societies, the National Research Council's Committee on Science and Mathematics Teacher Preparation (CSMTP) has determined that fundamental restructuring of

---

[1]With the recent release of standards from the International Technology Education Association (ITEA) (2000), teaching and learning about the history and roles of technology in modern society are likely to become increasingly important. Thus, although the authoring committee of this report is called the Committee on Science and Mathematics Teacher Preparation, its report places technology education on the same footing with science and mathematics education. Including consideration of the emerging subject area of technology also is consistent with the NRC's Statement of Task to the committee.

The new technology standards do not specifically address or offer recommendations about educating teachers in this subject area. Hence, new research and recommendations will be required to determine the most effective ways to teach and learn about technology. In addition, because there has been little if any consensus about appropriate ways to teach about technology prior to the release of these standards, little research has been undertaken about effective teaching and learning in this subject area. Therefore, the vast majority of references discussed in this report focus on science and mathematics.

teacher preparation and professional development is needed to best serve the interest of students' learning and of their future success as individuals, workers, and citizens. The committee also has concluded that such change is in the best interest of teachers of science and mathematics themselves, who, quite incontrovertibly, are not accorded the respect and recognition due professionals who hold such responsible positions in our society.

Increasing expectations under national, state, and local content standards are raising the stakes for what K-12 students need to know and to be able to do in science and mathematics. Concomitantly, expectations have risen for what K-12 teachers need to know and to be able to do. These expectations are reflected in part by bolstered state requirements for the type of postsecondary education and degrees required of new teachers.

Most instructors of these new teachers—including postsecondary faculty in science, mathematics, engineering, technology, and education— have not been able to provide the type of education that K-12 teachers need to succeed in their own classrooms. Numerous studies and the results from a variety of the Praxis and other teacher licensing and certification examinations demonstrate that many teachers, especially those who will teach in grades K-8,

do not have sufficient content knowledge or adequate background for teaching these subject areas. Indeed, in some states, middle school teachers (typically, grades 6-8) with generalist backgrounds are being assigned to teach science or mathematics exclusively. Many faculty in science, mathematics, engineering, and technology (SME&T) at the nation's colleges and universities may not be sufficiently aware of these changing expectations to provide the appropriate type and level of instruction needed by students who would be teachers. Nor do most of these faculty have the kinds of professional development experiences in teaching that would enable them to model effectively the kinds of pedagogy that are needed for success in grade K-12 classrooms. Similarly, some faculty in schools or colleges of education, especially those who are engaged with graduate programs, may have had little or no recent direct contact with teachers in classroom environments.

Once teachers reach the classroom, they often do not receive the support they need to keep their pedagogical skills and content knowledge current. Unlike in other professions, in education, few specific requirements and even fewer opportunities exist for teachers to engage in meaningful professional development (often called inservice education). Whereas other professions expect their practitioners to pursue advanced programs of study that increase and broaden their specific competencies for the profession, in education, most state regulations require only that teachers obtain post-baccalaureate credits or a master's degree within a certain period of time after being hired and then earn additional credits every few years thereafter. Content areas typically are not specified. These kinds of amorphous requirements for teachers may actually reduce the number of experienced teachers in classrooms, since many teachers who continue with their education pursue degrees in educational administration, allowing them to take better paying jobs outside of the classroom. In sum, current expectations for continuing education may not contribute to the retention of experienced teachers. In addition, recruitment and retention of high-quality teachers, especially those who are qualified to teach science and mathematics, has become a problem in some school districts across the country, especially where numerous professional opportunities exist not only outside of teaching but outside of education.

Unlike in teaching, in many other professions, coherent, well-recognized procedures and policies have been developed to attract, educate, and place professionals. Many of these other professions not only also expect their practitioners to upgrade their knowledge and skills throughout their careers but also have in place an enabling continuing education system. Importantly, most other professions do not view those who have recently entered the profession as being fully qualified or expert. Rather, there are full expectations that neophytes will continue to learn and grow through participation in regular professional development programs and as a result of mentoring by more senior colleagues. This trend is now infiltrating teaching; beginning teachers are sometimes now referred to as "competent novices" (for example, Schempp et al., 1998).

In addition, performance standards exist for many professions, often developed and maintained by members of those professions through accrediting boards and professional societies. Professionals who meet or exceed the standards are rewarded in tangible and appropriate ways. Although such guidelines exist for the teaching profession (for example, as developed in 1994 for practicing teachers by the National Board for Professional Teaching Standards and in 2000 by the National Council for Accreditation of Teacher Education), to date only a few of these guidelines have been incorporated systematically into the fabric and culture of the teaching profession.

THE EVIDENCE THAT HIGH-QUALITY TEACHING MATTERS

As noted in the extensive body of evidence cited throughout this report, research is confirming that good teaching does matter. In reviewing the literature, the Committee on Science and Mathematics Teacher Preparation (CSMTP) found that studies conducted over the past quarter century increasingly point to a strong correlation between student achievement in K-12 science and mathematics and the teaching quality and level of knowledge of K-12 teachers of science and mathematics. Other studies have found positive correlations between teachers' performance on state examinations, years of teaching experience, and advanced degrees and student tests scores in reading and mathematics. Specific content preparation of teachers also has been found to make a difference in student achievement. Several studies conducted over the past 15 years and detailed in the committee's report have concluded that "in-field" teachers—i.e., teachers holding specific certificates in certain subject areas—not only know more content in their subject area than their "out-of-field" colleagues but also use their content knowledge more effectively in the classroom.

Teaching effectiveness, defined as the ability to produce desired changes within the classroom, has been found to relate positively to the number of education courses taken by teachers, their grades as student teachers, and teaching experience. Some recent studies also have found that teacher quality accounts for a greater amount of the variance in student achievement than do variables such as the racial composition of schools or students' economic levels.

The CSMTP believes that these and other studies have clear implications for teacher preparation. Science and mathematics educators as well as practitioners have concluded that content knowledge must be a central focus of a science or mathematics teacher's preparation, with the result being a deeper understanding of the fundamental science, mathematics, or technology that he or she will need to teach. These conclusions are consistent with an emerging body of research in cognitive science that is contributing to our understanding of the processes by which people learn.

TEACHER EDUCATION AS A PROFESSIONAL CONTINUUM

Many national organizations have recommended improvements in the education of teachers of K-12 science and mathematics, including the National

Association of Biology Teachers (1990), the National Council of Teachers of Mathematics (1991), the Mathematical Association of America (1991), the National Board for Professional Teaching Standards (1994), the National Science Foundation (1996, 1998), the National Research Council (1996a, 1997a,b), the Association for the Education of Teachers of Science (1997), the National Science Teachers Association (1998), the American Institute of Physics (1999), and the Conference Board of the Mathematical Sciences (in preparation).

In recently released teacher education standards, the Interstate New Teacher Assessment and Support Consortium (INTASC, formed by the Council of Chief State School Officers) has specified that teachers of K-12 science and mathematics need to meet the National Research Council's standards for science and the National Council of Teachers of Mathematics' standards for mathematics. INTASC has emphasized further that teacher education should focus understanding of content in subject areas and knowing how to apply that understanding in problem-solving and inquiry-based situations in the classroom. More than 30 states now belong to INTASC.

Based on its review of the literature and of the recommendations of professional organizations, the CSMTP has concluded that teacher preparation

must be seen in the future as much more continual and seamless than it is today. The college education that leads to initial certification to teach (also known as preservice education) should be viewed as only the first part of a complex, career-long learning process that involves continual intellectual growth both inside and outside the classroom.

Standards for K-12 teaching coupled with increasing demands for improved teacher quality have created unprecedented opportunities for all players in the education community (with input and cooperation from the larger community, including industrial and research scientists and mathematicians) to design and implement new collaborative approaches to teacher education. In fact, over the past 10 years, many institutions have begun to develop such collaboration, often called a Professional Development School (PDS). Throughout the report, the committee has used this term to describe an intentional partnership between a college or university and the K-12 sector for teacher education and the improvement of teaching and learning in the schools. Although the objectives and infrastructures of PDS arrangements can vary widely, the committee found that some PDS models have become living laboratories for observation, experimentation, and extended practice—sites where teachers, students, and college and university faculty create new knowledge about effective teaching and experiment with, evaluate, and revise teaching practices.

Like student learning, teacher learning and professional development are part of an extremely long and complex process. Thus, a PDS encourages educators to restructure teacher education comprehensively, as opposed to incrementally and in a series of disjointed reforms. The PDS provides more systematic teaching experiences for preservice and novice teachers, where content and pedagogy are integrated and where teacher education takes place in environments that more closely resemble the classrooms in which these future teachers will work. At present, there are more than 1,000 PDS models in the United States, with some institutions of higher education exploring several different models. Examples of such partnerships are provided in Appendix E of the report.

The committee has concluded that when the partners in these kinds of collaboratives establish mechanisms for making decisions that are mutually supportive and collegial and when they

invest the time and money needed to sustain the partnership, they can improve the quality of teacher education and teaching in general. The committee's vision to improve teacher education that builds on the PDS approach is detailed in Chapter 6. Specific recommendations to various stakeholder communities are provided in Chapter 7.

VISION AND RECOMMENDATIONS

Vision

After examining what is known about the effectiveness of the PDS approach, the committee concluded that the entire professional community's[2] level of commitment to and input in both individual schools and districts can have significant effects on student achievement. Systemic support from the larger community in which a school is located also can make a critical difference in the success of teachers and their students (Smith and O'Day, 1991). This larger community includes policymakers, superintendents, district administrators, teacher unions, faculty and administra-

---

[2]The professional community includes all individuals and organizations that should be responsible for preparing, providing professional development for, and supporting teachers throughout their careers. Recent efforts to improve teacher education and professionalism must involve members of the K-12, higher education (including both two- and four-year colleges and universities), and business and industry communities.

tors from local colleges and universities, individual school staff, and parents. It also includes scientists and mathematicians outside of academe, who can bring their understanding and everyday applications of science and mathematics concepts and skills to K-12 teaching and learning improvement.

The approaches taken by PDSs, the vast body of literature that is reported and analyzed here, and the many examples of effective teacher education programs and policies and practices of other professions in the United States reviewed for this report by the CSMTP led committee members to develop a vision for a new type of partnership for teacher education. In the committee's vision (articulated in Chapter 6), the various communities involved with specific aspects of teacher education work much more closely together toward common goals. The current separation of programs to educate prospective and practicing teachers lessens considerably to the point of becoming a seamless continuum. Institutions that collaborate in these partnerships re-examine and, in some cases, redefine their roles in teacher education. The ultimate goal of the partnerships under the committee's vision is to offer teachers ongoing opportunities to improve their understanding of the subjects they teach, the ways they teach, and their standing as professionals.

It was in this regard, then, that the committee took particular note of the partnerships between medical schools and their teaching hospitals that involve collaboration between teaching and clinical faculty in the education of new generations of physicians. The committee emphasizes that the primary goal of any partnership arrangement would be to improve teacher education in ways that contribute to enhanced student learning and achievement.

In reflecting on its findings and conclusions, the CSMTP established the following six guiding principles on which further action to improve K-12 teacher education in science, mathematics, and technology should be based:

1. The improvement of teacher education and teaching in science, mathematics, and technology should be viewed as a top national priority.

2. Teacher education in science, mathematics, and technology must become a career-long process. High-quality professional development programs that include intellectual growth as well as the upgrading of teachers' knowledge and skills must be expected and essential features in the careers of all teachers.

3. Through changes in the rewards for, incentives for, and expectations of teachers, teaching as a profession must be upgraded in status and

stature to the level of other professions.

4. Both individually and collectively, two- and four-year colleges and universities must assume greater responsibility and be held more accountable for improving teacher education.

5. Neither the higher education nor the K-12 communities can successfully improve teacher education as effectively in isolation as they can by working closely together. Collective, fully integrated efforts among school staff and administrators in individual schools and districts, teacher unions, faculty and administrators in institutions of higher education, policymakers from local colleges and universities, parents, and the private sector are essential for addressing these issues.

6. Many more scientists, mathematicians, and engineers must become well informed enough to become involved with local and national

efforts to provide the appropriate content knowledge and pedagogy of their disciplines to current and future teachers.[3]

To initiate action based on these principles, the committee envisions a new partnership arrangement between K-12 schools and the higher education community, with support and assistance from the broader community, that is designed to promote high-quality teacher education over the continuum of a teacher's career. Two- and four-year colleges and universities, and especially those that have teacher education programs, would enter into long-term partnerships with one or more school districts. Large school districts could partner with more than one institution of higher education (for example, with their local community college and a four-year institution). The objectives of such partnerships would include the sharing of responsibility for teacher preparation and providing on-going

---

[3]In a recent study of Columbia University's Summer Research Program for Science School Teachers, Silverstein (2000) found that students of teachers who had participated in summer research received higher scores and pass rates on the New York State Regents Examination than the students of teachers from the same schools who did not participate in such programs (teachers who participated in this program were drawn from a broad spectrum of schools in the New York City area). Additionally, participation in Westinghouse/Intel Talent Search projects, science clubs, and extra-curricular activities in science was higher for students whose teachers participated in this program compared to students from the same schools whose teachers did not participate. Additional information about this program is available at <http://cpmcnet.columbia.edu/dept/physio/>. The program at Columbia University is one of approximately 70 such programs across the U.S. that are part of the Science Work Experiences for Teachers(SWEPT. A listing of SWEPT programs is available at <http://cpmcnet.columbia.edu/dept/physio/swep.html>.

professional development for the school districts' teachers.[4] The committee envisions that each of the contributors and stakeholders in these partnerships would be recognized and utilized for their particular professional expertise in science, mathematics, and technology education. The partners would work collectively toward improving teaching and ongoing professional development for all teachers in the partnership community, including those in higher education. These partnerships collectively would establish and implement goals for improving the learning and academic achievements in science, mathematics, and technology of students in affiliated institutions, including students in teacher education programs and the children in the schools that are members of the partnerships.

It is important to note that this new type of partnership envisioned by the committee would involve a restructuring of the various phases of teacher education. Responsibility for student teaching experiences would be vested primarily in school districts that participate in the partnership. In turn, professional development would fall primarily within the purview of the higher education partners. The committee's vision also would involve a corresponding rethinking of how each partner uses its resources in support of the partnership.

Thus, in the new teacher education partnership envisioned in this report, master teachers in partner school districts could have adjunct faculty appointments in the partner two- and four-year colleges or universities. These teachers would take on a much more significant role in the mentoring of future teachers during their practicum experiences. In turn, faculty in both the school of education and in science, mathematics, and engineering departments at partner colleges and universities would assume much greater responsibility for providing ongoing professional development opportunities for the school districts' teachers. The partnerships would base their approaches to improved teacher education on the scholarly literature, recommendations about improving teacher education from professional and disciplinary organizations, and an ongoing analysis and evaluation of the partnership itself. A major component of this evaluation would be the academic

---

[4]The committee emphasizes in this report that all colleges and universities, including those that do not have formal teacher education programs, should become more involved with improving teacher education because the nation's teacher workforce consists of many individuals who have matriculated at all types of two- and four-year institutions of higher education. Although many of these schools do not offer formal teacher education programs, virtually every institution of higher education, through the kinds of courses it offers, the teaching it models, and the advising it provides to students, has the potential to influence whether or not its graduates will pursue careers in teaching.

achievement in science, mathematics, and technology of the students in the schools that are members of the partnership. The partnerships also might undertake directed research within the member organizations to find ways to improve further teacher education and student outcomes in science, mathematics, and technology. Faculty in schools of education could play an especially critical role in directing some of their research efforts to evaluating systemically the efficacy of teacher education programs in these partnerships.

The committee acknowledges that achieving this vision will not be straightforward, easily accomplished, or inexpensive. It will require fundamental rethinking and restructuring of the relationships between the K-12 and higher education communities in SME&T, including financial relationships. It also will require fundamental revamping of teaching as a profession.

GENERAL RECOMMENDATIONS

The CSMTP recommends that

1. Teacher education in science, mathematics, and technology be viewed as a continuum of programs and professional experiences that enables individuals to move seamlessly from college preparation for teaching to careers in teaching these subject areas.

2. Teacher education be viewed as a career-long process that allows teachers of science, mathematics, and technology to acquire and regularly update the content knowledge and pedagogical tools needed to teach in ways that enhance student learning and achievement in these subjects.

3. Teacher education be structured in ways that allow teachers to grow individually in their profession and to contribute to the further enhancement of both teaching and their disciplines.

As outlined, then detailed in its vision, the CSMTP believes that the goals and objectives of these general recommendations can be achieved by all two- and four-year colleges and universities (those with and without programs in teacher education) working with school districts to establish partnerships for teacher education.

SPECIFIC RECOMMENDATIONS

The CSMTP further offers the following specific recommendations:

For Governments

Local, state, and federal governments should recognize and acknowledge the need to improve teacher education in science and mathematics, as well as assist the public in understanding and supporting improvement. Governments should understand that restructuring teacher education will require large infusions of financial support and make a strong commitment to provide the direct and indirect funding required to support local and regional partnerships for improving teacher education in these disciplines.[5] They also should encourage the recruitment and retention of teachers of science and mathematics—particularly those who are "in-field"—through financial incentives, such as salaries that are commensurate and competitive with those in other professions in science, mathematics, and technology; low-interest student loans; loan forgiveness for recently certified teachers in these disciplines who commit to teaching; stipends for teaching internships; and grants to teachers, school districts, or teacher education partnerships to offset the costs of continual professional development.

For Collaboration Between Institutions of Higher Education and the K-12 Community

Two- and four-year institutions of higher education and school districts that are involved with partnerships for teacher education should—working together—establish a comprehensive, integrated system of recruiting and advising people who are interested in teaching science, mathematics, and technology.

For the Higher Education Community

1. Science, mathematics, and engineering departments at two- and four-year colleges and universities should assume greater responsibility for offering college-level courses that provide teachers with strong exposure to appropriate content and that model the kinds of pedagogical

---

[5]A recent survey by the National Science Teachers Association (NSTA) has concluded that nearly 40 percent of science teachers in the United States are considering leaving their jobs. The primary reason cited was job dissatisfaction, with low pay and lack of support from principals the most likely causes of this dissatisfaction (*Education Week,* April 19, 2000). A report from the Texas State Teachers Association pointed to similar levels of dissatisfaction among teachers in that state (Henderson, 2000). In comparison, for all subject areas, nearly 20 percent of 1992-93 teacher graduates who entered public school teaching in 1993-94 had left the profession within three years. The brightest novice teachers, as measured by their college-entrance exams, were the most likely to leave. Teachers who did not participate in an induction program, who were dissatisfied with student discipline, or who were unhappy with the school environment were much more likely to leave than their peers (*Education Week*, 2000).

approaches appropriate for teaching that content.

2. Two- and four-year colleges and universities should reexamine and redesign introductory college-level courses in science and mathematics to better accommodate the needs of practicing and future teachers.

3. Universities whose primary mission includes education research should set as a priority the development and execution of peer-reviewed research studies that focus on ways to improve teacher education, the art of teaching, and learning for people of all ages. New research that focuses broadly on synthesizing data across studies and linking it to school practice in a wide variety of school settings would be especially helpful to the improvement of teacher education and professional development for both prospective and experienced teachers. The results of this research should be collated and disseminated through a national electronic database or library.

4. Two- and four-year colleges and universities should maintain contact with and provide guidance to teachers who complete their preparation and development programs.

5. Following a period of collaborative planning and preparation, two- and four-year colleges and universities in a partnership for teacher educa-tion should assume primary respon-sibility for providing professional development opportunities to experienced teachers of science, mathematics, and technology. Such programs would involve faculty from science, mathematics, and engineer-ing disciplines and from schools of education.

For the K-12 Education Community

1. Following a period of collaborative planning and preparation, school districts in a partnership for teacher education should assume primary responsibility for providing high-quality practicum experiences and internships for prospective teachers.

2. School districts in a partnership for teacher education should assume primary responsibility for developing and overseeing field experiences, student teaching, and internship programs for new teachers of science, mathematics, and technology.

3. School districts should collaborate with two- and four-year colleges and universities to provide professional development opportunities to experienced teachers of science, mathematics, and technology. Such programs would involve faculty from science, mathematics, and engineer-ing disciplines and from schools of education. Teachers who participate

in these programs would, in turn, offer their expertise and guidance to others involved with the partnership.

For Professional and Disciplinary Organizations

1. Organizations that represent institutions of higher education should assist their members in establishing programs to help new teachers. For example, databases of information about new teachers could be developed and shared among member institutions so that colleges and universities could be notified when a newly certified teacher was moving to their area to teach. Those colleges and universities could then plan and offer welcoming and support activities, such as opportunities for continued professional and intellectual growth.

2. Professional disciplinary societies in science, mathematics, and engineering, higher education organizations, government at all levels, and business and industry should become more engaged as partners (as opposed to advisors or overseers) in efforts to improve teacher education.

3. Professional disciplinary societies in science, mathematics, and engineering, and higher education organizations also should work together to align their policies and recommendations for improving teacher education in science, mathematics, and technology.

These recommendations are elaborated in Chapter 7.

1
Introduction and Context

Nearly everyone can drive a car. But can everyone drive a tractor-trailer or fly an airliner? What minimum qualifications and background are required to carry out these demanding tasks competently? How does one define an "expert" in each of these categories? How much training and experience would travelers want the truck driver or pilot to have had?

These kinds of questions were raised recently in an article comparing methods used around the world for the training of commercial airline pilots for United States and foreign carriers (Mangan, 2000). Pilots for the U.S.-based airlines go through training over a six-year period that includes a four-year college degree (or military piloting experience). They then move through the ranks from flight instructor to pilot of a regional carrier. By contrast, new pilots for many foreign carriers are given one year of rigorous training and instruc-

tion. Which training method is preferable? The foreign carrier pilots do not appear to have more accidents, but they also do not have the experience and flexibility that results from a longer-term training program.

Like pilots who fly aircraft and are responsible for cargo, crew, and passengers, teachers have demanding jobs, with responsibilities that can have long-term impacts on their students, communities, and society in general. Thus, as with the skills required of airline pilots, one might reasonably ask, "Can everyone teach?" The answer to this is likely "Yes!" That is, virtually everyone has taught something to someone else, even if it was as a parent or friend. "Teaching as telling" is a common human behavior. But what does it require to be a highly competent teacher in a classroom?

In the prevailing cultural norms in the United States, there seems to be an assumption that certain professions do not require all that much background—that anyone can be a professional writer, for example, or teacher, with the relative outcomes the same regardless of education, experience, or professional development. But as this report will show, highly knowledgeable, highly skilled teachers do make a difference in terms of student learning. And, therefore, if for no other reason, careful attention must be paid to how they are educated and professionally supported and nurtured throughout their careers.

THE REFORM MOVEMENT IN EDUCATION: CURRENT CHALLENGES

Although education has been a central focus of concern for the U.S. public for many years, the first contemporary national expression of concern was issued in 1983, in a U.S. Department of Education-funded report entitled *A Nation at Risk* (National Commission on Excellence in Education). That report warned of a "rising tide of mediocrity" that threatened the United States both economically and militarily. At the time, the nation was especially concerned with the rise of Japanese economic power and Soviet military might. Sixteen years later, the United States stands as the world's sole economic and military superpower, but our nation still

remains concerned about the academic performance of U.S. children on national (e.g., National Assessment of Educational Progress—NAEP) and international (e.g., the Third International Mathematics Science Study—TIMSS)

The key difference between the current and previous calls for reform in teacher preparation is a focus on strategies that coordinate the preparation of high quality teachers with improvements in K-12 student achievement.

Rodriguez, 1998

---

assessments compared with the academic performance of students in many other countries. What might these poor performances bode for our future international and economic stature? Are schools accomplishing what we want for our children? For *all* of our children?

Following publication and national discussion of *A Nation at Risk*, a spate of other reports appeared. Those reports offered criticisms of and proposed solutions for the entire landscape of K-12 education (e.g., reviewed by Darling-Hammond, 1997). In science and mathematics, the American Association for the Advancement of Science (AAAS) initiated its comprehensive project, "Project 2061"[1] in 1986. Project 2061 resulted in the publication of *Science for All Americans* (1989), which articulated AAAS' vision for scientific literacy. *Benchmarks for Science Literacy*, which offered goals and objectives for what U.S. students should know and be able to do in science, appeared in 1993. In 1986, the National Council of Teachers of Mathematics began its work on K-12 content standards for mathematics, which were released in 1989 and subsequently revised in 2000. By the end of the 1980s, the National Science Teachers Association (NSTA) had started crafting a new approach to teaching science (*Scope, Sequence and Coordination*), which recommended that students in grades 9-12 be exposed to every science subject each year (NSTA, 1996). In 1991, the National Research Council was asked by the president of the NSTA and other scientific organizations, the U.S. Department of Education, the National Science Foundation, and the co-chairs of the National Education Goals Panel (a project supported by the National Governors' Association) to coordinate the development of national science education standards. These

voluntary standards, published in 1996, reflected input from thousands of scientists, mathematicians, and science and mathematics educators. The *National Science Education Standards* addressed not only content but also critical related issues, such as the professionalism of teachers, the roles of colleges and universities in preparing teachers to implement and teach curricula that are consistent with the content standards, appropriate assessment of knowledge, and the educational infrastructure that would be needed to support these new approaches to teaching and learning.[2] The development of these national standards reflected the concern that U.S. students needed to become much more knowledgeable about science and mathematics than they had been in the past. The national standards presaged a growing researched-based consensus about how people learn and should be taught (summarized in NRC, 1999d,e).

All 50 states are now at varying stages of developing and implementing their own curriculum frameworks and learning outcomes for students in grades K-12 (Education Commission of the

---

[1]"Project 2061" was so named because it was launched in 1986, the year that Halley's comet made its most recent close pass by Earth. The next time that the comet returns will be in 2061. The title serves as a metaphor for what AAAS views as a generation of change for fundamentally new approaches to teaching and learning science.

[2]In mathematics, the National Council of Teachers of Mathematics issued a separate set of recommendations for teacher education (NCTM, 1991) two years after the release of its content standards for mathematics.

States, 2000). Many of these state initiatives are based at least in part on the national standards. Thus, a growing consensus is emerging about the science and mathematics content that all students in grades K-12 should know, understand, and be able to do to prepare themselves for living and working in the 21st century.

While there continues to be a recognized need to improve the content of science and mathematics education for K-12 students, a near revolution in understanding human learning has been taking place through the emerging field of cognitive science. This research, summarized recently by a study committee of the National Research Council (1999d), indicates that teachers should incorporate content-appropriate methods of teaching that improve their students' chances of knowing and understanding content in areas such as mathematics. This new understanding, coupled with research that substantiates the importance of guiding beginning teachers so that they learn to employ a variety of instructional practices, implies the need for and benefit of sound preparation in both subject matter and pedagogical training for prospective teachers (Stoddard and Floden, 1995; Ball, 1997).

Concomitant with the reform of content in K-12 science and mathematics and knowledge about how people learn, there have been calls for restructuring teacher preparation and professional development. The leading proponents of education reform have argued that the attainment of high standards for students—standards that demand understanding and the ability to perform—will be unlikely until teachers are educated in ways that enable them to implement and teach curricula that are consistent with the vision, goals, and content of the national standards. If children are to be able to engage in inquiry and problem solving as they learn science and mathematics, then surely their teachers also need to experience and practice inquiry and problem solving in their own education (NRC, 2000a).

Three other recent reports have served to catalyze attempts to improve teacher education:

• In 1996, the Council of Basic Education (CBE) cited several problems that it claimed compromised the education of teachers. These problems included inadequate and poorly supervised school-based practicum experience, the mediocre academic credentials of students who enroll in teacher education programs, and the questionable quality of faculty in the schools of education who prepare those students (Rigden, 1996).

• In the same year, a report from the

National Commission on Teaching and America's Future (NCTAF, 1996) admonished educators of teachers for not attending to problems of uninspired teaching in their own courses, a curriculum that lacks both substance and depth, and a lack of coherence and articulation in teacher education programs between schools of education and other disciplines. Although critical about how teachers are prepared, the NCTAF report also pointed to research data showing that the United States labors with fatal distractions in its reform efforts, including the misguided beliefs that 1) anyone can teach, especially if they have adequate content knowledge, and that 2) teacher preparation programs contribute little to the production of qualified teachers and high-quality teaching.

In a second report, NCTAF (1997) cited 12 partner states that have begun far-reaching sets of reforms that could affect virtually all aspects of teaching. In North Carolina, for example, the state's Excellent Schools Act of 1997 enacted "nearly all of the recommendations of the National Commission that were not already in place in the state," including increasing teachers' average salaries by 33 percent over four years; improving teacher education by establishing school-university partnerships to create clinical school settings and requiring special education training for all newly prepared teachers; enhancing mentoring of beginning teachers by setting standards for the selection of mentor teachers and providing funds to professionally prepare and compensate mentors; and the funding of professional development tied to state content standards for students.

• Mundry et al. (1999) noted the lack of focus and coherence in teacher education programs. That study also highlighted the failure of teacher educators to establish a "coherent set or 'continuum' of career-long learning experiences for all K-12 teachers of science and mathematics, primarily to improve teaching and learning in the classroom." Significant effort is needed to bridge the gap between preservice and inservice teacher education. However, the authors noted that a "disconnect" in teacher education programs actually stems from a major problem that teacher educators face. In the current education system, most teachers do not have access to high-quality, *ongoing* opportunities for professional development. Thus, schools of education attempt to prepare prospective teachers for the demands of the present system of K-12 education as well as for both probable and unanticipated changes to the education system in the future. Partly as a result of these attempts to cover such broad ground in teacher preparation programs, many graduates and their supervisors report that their teacher preparation programs were inadequate, idealistic, or too theoretical.

Too often, teacher preparation programs are characterized by a lack of coherence and articulation across the general education, science education, and professional education curriculum strands. In each of these three areas, expectations typically are defined by a list of courses. These courses in turn usually are defined by a body of basic knowledge within the respective disciplines without major attention to the nature of the investigative modes that produced them. Similarly, few courses address the application of this knowledge to societal issues or other matters—dimensions that the Standards say need significant attention in K-12 education in science.

National Research Council, 1997b

In the past decade, the criticism of teacher preparation programs also has extended to content preparation. Numerous reports, including those from the American Association for the Advancement of Science (1990) and the National Research Council (1989, 1991, 1995, 1999h) have criticized the nearly exclusive use of lecture-based teaching that prospective teacher candidates experience in many of their undergraduate science and mathematics courses. As noted in the *National Science Education Standards* (NRC, 1996a), science is not something that is done to students, it is something that students do. If teachers are to implement standards-based teaching approaches, then they too must experience these models of instruction in their undergraduate classes. Furthermore, prospective teachers need to experience science and mathematics learning through inquiry, problem-based approaches, and direct, hands-on experiences in the classroom, laboratory, and field (e.g., Howard Hughes Medical Institute, 1996; NRC, 1999h).

Although calls for reform persist, teacher educators at some major research universities have been working for many years to reform teacher education. Representatives from many of these universities banded together in 1986 to produce the hallmark Holmes Group Report (Holmes Group, 1986). This report was to be the first in a series of efforts to deal with the reform and revitalization of teacher education. The Holmes report called for prospective teachers to acquire a solid background in the liberal arts as undergraduates and then to engage in substantive post-

Teaching science through inquiry allows students to conceptualize a question and then seek possible explanations that respond to that question. For example, in my field of cell biology, cell membranes have to be selectively permeable—they have to let foodstuffs like sugars pass inward and wastes like carbon dioxide pass out, while holding the many big molecules that from the cell inside. What kind of material could have these properties and yet be able to expand as the cell grows?

It is certainly easy to remember another and more familiar type of science teaching from my childhood. In this approach—which remains depressingly common today—teachers provide their students with sets of science facts and with technical words to describe those facts. In the worst case, this type of science teaching assumes that education consists of filling a student's head with vocabulary words and associations, such as mitochondria being "the powerhouses of the cell," DNA being the "genetic material," and motion producing "kinetic energy." Science classes of this type treat education as if it were preparation for a quiz show or a game of trivial pursuit.

This view of science education has many problems. Most students are not interested in being quiz show participants. They fail to see how this type of knowledge will be useful to them in the future. They therefore lack the motivation for this kind of "school learning."

Most important, this kind of teaching misses a tremendous opportunity to give all students the problem-solving skills that they will need to be effective workers and citizens in the 21st century.

Bruce Alberts
Excerpted from the Foreword in
National Research Council (2000b)

baccalaureate work that would allow them to apply their knowledge and pedagogical skills in school settings. The Holmes report also urged that teacher education take place at "teaching centers" linked to major universities, a strategy parallel to the reform of medical education in the early 1900s following publication of the Flexner Report (1910).

A major study by Goodlad (1994) served as further impetus for restructuring teacher education. Goodlad highlighted significant problems, such as the lack of "connectedness" among schools of education, university liberal arts programs, and the K-12 education sector. Goodlad also cited as problematic the low status accorded to teacher education programs and schools of education on university campuses. He recommended strengthening the connections between reform efforts taking place in schools of education (teacher preparation) and those in K-12 education (e.g., implementation of content standards). Both the Holmes Group and Goodlad reports encouraged development of Professional Development Schools and other forms of university and K-12 partnerships. More than 300 schools of education responded to these reports to create programs that go beyond the traditional four-year degree programs to include more extensive study of subject matter and more

extensive clinical training in K-12 schools (Darling-Hammond, 1997). In 1998, Abdal-Haqq reported that over 600 PDS models had been developed in the United States, with some of these institutions exploring several different models for improving teacher education. More than 1,000 such schools exist today (Abdal-Haqq, personal communication). Professional Development Schools are described in greater detail later in this report.

ROADBLOCKS TO CHANGES IN TEACHER EDUCATION

Murray (1996) emphasized that a significant barrier to the reform of teacher education results from a long-standing belief among many people that teaching is a natural human endeavor. Parents teach their children, and friends and colleagues teach each other. Even people with few personal connections or similar interests may teach each other. However, in most of these cases, the act of teaching almost always occurs among people of like minds, backgrounds, education, or beliefs and centers around tasks or problems that the teacher and learner have in common. It is strikingly different from what typically occurs in schools.

The notion that anyone can teach clearly is ingrained in the contemporary culture of the United States, and it can be seen in how university professors are prepared and selected (Merseth, 1993; Murray, 1996). The typical doctorate program emphasizes research, not teaching. Yet many of these researchers take positions at colleges or universities where they also must teach. Many reports in recent years have called for paying more attention to teaching, especially of undergraduates (reviewed in NRC, 1999h; Rothman and Narum, 1999).

These notions that "teaching is telling" and that "anyone can teach" also are seen in the design of many alternative teacher education programs that emphasize content background and de-emphasize lengthy pedagogical preparation. These programs might, for example, actively recruit college graduates, provide a highly abbreviated "training" period on pedagogy, and then immerse the novice teachers in the culture of the classroom, sometimes with a mentor and sometimes not.

Sadly, the belief that anyone can teach also seems to be reflected in some traditional teacher preparation programs. This notion or belief that everyone can teach can lead to overly simplistic approaches to teaching and teacher education. The design of such programs seems to presume that all teacher candidates have some level of natural teaching ability, that teaching is largely "telling," and that the primary role of teacher educators is to acquaint their students with procedural rules that will ensure success in the classroom. Thus, some teacher education programs stress to their students "basic principles of teaching" and then help these teacher candidates learn, practice, and implement them (e.g., Goodlad, 1990; Howey, 1996).

Such approaches also can lead to the espousal of "simple" solutions to problems such as maintaining classroom discipline rather than to broader, deeper examination of what may be the underlying causes for disciplinary problems—failed instruction. Thus, those programs may lack program coherence or a comprehensive philosophical framework. They may not integrate preparation in subject content and pedagogy. Field components of the program may be instituted primarily to comply with state regulations for certifying teachers or for accreditation of the program itself. All of the aforementioned attributes of some traditional preparation programs may help explain why the preparation of teachers historically has been described as teacher "training" rather than teacher "education" (Goodlad, 1994; Howey, 1996; Mundry et al., 1999).

Career-long professional development for teachers has suffered a similar lack of coherence, integration, and continuity. In the current system, school districts typically have assumed primary responsibility for inservice education. These programs too often are presented in the form of short (typically one-day) "workshops" that may not be sufficiently focused or grounded in practice to be useful to teachers. Or, teachers are sent to a teachers' convention where they may attend or participate in sessions on a variety of related or unrelated topics, collecting teaching ideas that school officials hope they will be able to implement shortly after returning to their classrooms or share with teacher colleagues. If their content and pedagogical preparation has modeled teaching as a simple, straightforward enterprise—"teaching as telling"—then these teachers' students may not be better off as a result of these kinds of inservice experiences. More than small changes, what is needed are fundamental changes in teachers' content and pedagogical preparation and ongoing professional development (Ball, 1997; Loucks-Horsley et al., 1998).

INCREASING EXPECTATIONS FOR TEACHING AND LEARNING

The paradigm for teacher education outlined above was developed in and may have worked during an era when students and classes were more homogeneous and when the level of knowledge required of students was more basic. The approaches to teacher preparation described above and the patterns of inservice programs met the needs of a largely agrarian society and also worked later when schools were expected to prepare "citizen-students" to function as workers in an increasingly industrialized society. But current learning goals include expectations for much higher levels of knowledge and understanding about science (AAAS, 1993; NRC, 1996a), mathematics (NCTM, 1989, 2000), and technology (ITEA, 2000). In addition, these standards emphasize understanding as well as knowing content and the ability to undertake activities that are related to these disciplines. For example, the *National Science Education Standards* (NRC, 1996a)[3] call for teachers of science to

- plan inquiry-based programs for their students.
- guide and facilitate learning.
- engage in on-going assessment that is appropriate for the new expectations for learning.
- design and manage learning environments.
- develop communities of science learners.

---

[3]An elaboration of these six teaching standards can be found in Appendix A.

- actively participate in the ongoing planning and development of the school science program.

Similarly, the NCTM's *Professional Standards for Teaching Mathematics* (1991)[4] envision teachers as decision-makers who must bring to their classrooms the following:

- A deep content knowledge and understanding of mathematics beyond the mathematics they are teaching.
- An understanding of students as learners and their previous and current knowledge about the subject area.
- Carefully selected learning goals.
- Knowledge of a variety of pedagogical strategies, including the use of modeling and simulation.
- Experience knowing how to frame questions, choose activities to address misunderstandings they know students have, and assess student learning appropriately.

According to the new *Principles and Standards for School Mathematics*, effective mathematics teachers use strategies and approaches that range from extended student explorations in small groups to direct teaching. As student needs change, teachers make deliberate shifts among these strategies.

Teaching mathematics well "takes deep insight about mathematics, about teaching, and about learners, coupled with a sound and robust mathematics curriculum and thoughtful reflection and planning" (NCTM, 2000).

Linked with these standards for teaching is changing expectations about what should receive greater emphasis in science and mathematics instruction. Table 1-1 is an example from the *National Science Education Standards* that illustrates these differences.

Both the science and mathematics standards call for teachers to ensure that all students have learning opportunities in science and mathematics that result in measurable learning outcomes (NRC, 1996a; NCTM, 2000). However, today's K-12 student population in the United States is much more diverse, in terms of different languages, cultures, and ethnicities, for example, than it was just a few decades ago, and teaching standards-based science and mathematics to this new generation of students can pose great educational challenges for teachers.

Expectations for increased performance by K-12 students have shifted dramatically during the past 10 years with the development and publication of standards and curriculum frameworks of individual states, many of which are

---

[4]An elaboration of these standards can be found in Appendix A.

TABLE 1-1 Changing Emphases and Expectations in Science Education

The *National Science Education Standards* envision change throughout the system. The teaching standards encompass the following changes in emphasis:

Less Emphasis on	More Emphasis on
Treating all students alike and responding to the group as a whole	Understanding and responding to individual student's interests, strengths, experiences, and needs
Rigidly following curriculum	Selecting and adapting curriculum
Focusing on student acquisition of information	Focusing on student understanding and use of scientific knowledge, ideas, and inquiry processes
Presenting scientific knowledge through lecture, text, and demonstration	Guiding students in active and extended scientific inquiry
Asking for recitation of acquired knowledge	Providing opportunities for scientific discussion and debate among students
Testing students for factual information at the end of the unit or chapter	Continuously assessing student understanding
Maintaining responsibility and authority	Sharing responsibility for learning with students
Supporting competition	Supporting a classroom community with cooperation, shared responsibility, and respect
Working alone	Working with other teachers to enhance the science program

based at least in part on the national statements of learning goals in science and mathematics. In increasing numbers of states, calls for higher student understanding of and achievement in science and mathematics has been coupled with high-stakes standardized tests, placing even greater pressure for effective teaching performance on teachers. These changing expectations are making clear that teaching no longer can be seen as an activity that anyone can do, nor is it primarily "teaching as telling." Rather, these developments must compel those who educate prospective and currently practicing teachers to redesign their programs to meet the needs of teachers in this new educational environment (Goodlad, 1994; Darling-Hammond, 1997).

ORIGINS OF THE STUDY

As part of a grant from the National Science Foundation (NSF), the National Research Council (NRC) commissioned in 1998 the Committee on Science and Mathematics Teacher Preparation (CSMTP).[5] This study committee has undertaken a series of projects and activities to examine ways to improve the education of teachers of science, mathematics, and technology for grades K-12. The Executive Committee of the NRC's Governing Board approved the following Statement of Task to define the nature and scope of the committee's purview and responsibilities:

> The [study committee] will identify critical issues emerging from existing

practices and policies for teacher preparation. The project report will synthesize existing research relevant to teacher preparation in science, mathematics, and technology. The process will include collecting and summarizing comprehensive recommendations that have been developed by professional societies for science, mathematics, and technology teacher preparation. These three components of the project report will be interwoven, so that the resulting report provides an analysis of the ways in which research, recommendations from professional societies, and practice might be integrated to improve the teacher preparation process in mathematics, science, and technology. (1998)

In response, this report of the committee explores the landscape of teacher education in general, and then focuses on issues that can be seen as specific or unique to the teaching of science, mathematics, and technology. It synthesizes and builds on the research literature and current calls for reform of K-16 science and mathematics education as well as on more general principles of effective teacher education that are derived from analysis of actual classroom practice. Research about what is

---

[5]As noted throughout this report, this study undertaken by the members of the Committee on Science and Mathematics Teacher Preparation has led to the conclusion that teacher preparation (which often is equated with the education of prospective teachers, or preservice education) cannot be addressed adequately by itself. Instead, teacher preparation must be viewed as a component of a much more integrated approach to improving the education of teachers at all stages of their careers. Thus, while the study committee was designated as the Committee on Science and Mathematics Teacher Preparation, this report stresses teacher education in its entirety rather than separating teacher preparation from professional development (also known as inservice education).

currently known about effective teacher preparation and career-long professional development undergirds the report's discussion, conclusions, and recommendations.

The main topics and issues contained in the report's chapters are

- The broader context and issues surrounding teaching and teacher education that led to the NRC's establishment of a Committee on Science and Mathematics Teacher Preparation (this chapter);
- The current status of education for teachers of science, mathematics, and technology, including stresses on current systems of teacher education and the teaching profession that are exacerbated by the urgent need in many localities for many new "qualified" teachers, especially in science, mathematics, and technology (Chapter 2);
- The critical importance of well-prepared teachers for improving student learning and achievement (Chapter 3);
- Descriptions of how teacher preparation might be redesigned in light of research, new knowledge about how teachers learn the content and art of their profession, and, based on recommendations from higher education organizations and the disciplines themselves, how expecta-

tions for the professional quality of teachers and teaching, especially for science and mathematics, are likely to change in the near future (Chapter 4);
- Descriptions of and vignettes from exemplary and promising current practices for improving teacher education in science, mathematics, and technology, including the establishment of close local or regional partnerships between school districts and teacher educators, scientists, and mathematicians in institutions of higher education (Chapter 5);
- The study committee's vision for improving teacher education in these disciplines (Chapter 6);
- Specific recommendations for implementing the committee's vision for the improvement of education for K-12 teachers of science, mathematics, and technology (Chapter 7); and
- Information about national standards for K-12 science and mathematics for teacher development, course and curriculum content, and teaching practices (Appendixes A-C); statewide programs that offer ongoing professional development for both novice and experienced teachers of K-12 science and mathematics (Appendix D); examples of formal partnerships between institutions of higher education and schools or school districts (Appendix E); and a glossary of terms specific to the profession.

The CSMTP's vision for improved teacher education (Chapter 6) and general as well as specific recommendations (Chapter 7) not only are grounded in research and reports of best practice in teacher education programs and classrooms but on advice from professional societies and organizations, as well. Therefore, committee members are confident that the report will prove useful to the many dedicated people who are working to improve the quality of the education of teachers of K-12 science, mathematics, and technology. The report also should help increase the numbers of teachers who are teaching in ways that allow their students to understand and appreciate the wonders of science, mathematics, and technology and the relevance of these disciplines to virtually every aspect of people's lives in the new millennium.

2
The Continuum of Teacher Education in Science, Mathematics, and Technology: Problems and Issues

What does it require to be a competent—or highly competent—teacher of science, mathematics, or technology?[1] Should we allow anyone to teach children in general or to teach children science, mathematics, or technology in particular, even though they might have only limited amounts of "training?" Are four years of education at the pre-baccalaureate level sufficient to produce competent teachers in these subject areas? How can professional development programs improve a teacher's effectiveness in the classroom? How should the quality of that teaching be defined and measured?

Calls for the reform of K-12 science and mathematics education and science and mathematics teacher education have been issued with increasing frequency by national and state leaders, policy-makers, and a plethora of education-related organizations. Some of these exhortations seem to be supported by data that point to the generally poor or only slightly above average academic performance of U.S. students in science and mathematics on international tests. Contextually, there are several related issues that must be taken into consideration in the improvement of teacher education.

---

[1]This report includes consideration of technology education. The members of the committee agree that, in addition to having an adequate foundation and understanding of science and mathematics, students must understand the role and nature of technology by itself as well as technology's relationship to the more traditional disciplines of science and mathematics. In April 2000, the International Technology Education Association (ITEA) released standards for technology education that provide guidance to educators about how to incorporate the teaching and learning about technology issues into the curriculum for grades K-12. However, because the kind of technology education being proposed by the ITEA standards is quite new, little research has been undertaken that addressed how specifically to improve it. Thus, most of the discussion of research data in this report necessarily focuses on the teaching and learning of science and mathematics.

TEACHER EDUCATION ISSUES

• **Research is demonstrating that good teaching does matter.** An increasing amount of research suggests that student achievement correlates with teaching quality and the level of knowledge of teachers in science and mathematics. However, numerous studies and the results from a variety of the Praxis and other teacher licensing and certification examinations demonstrate that many teachers, especially those who will teach in grades K-8 do not have sufficient content knowledge or adequate skills for teaching these disciplines.

• **In addition to benchmarks and standards for science, mathematics, and technology from national organizations (e.g., AAAS, 1993; NRC, 1996a; NCTM, 1989, 2000; ITEA, 2000; American Mathematical Association of Two-Year Colleges, 1995), most states have developed their own curriculum frameworks and expectations for learning outcomes in these subjects.**[2] However, it is clear that many of the nation's teachers are not adequately prepared to teach these subjects using standards-based approaches and in ways that bolster student learning and achievement.

• **The preparation of beginning teachers by many colleges and universities (preservice education) does not meet the needs of the modern classroom (e.g., American Council on Education, 1999; American Federation of Teachers, 2000).** Many states are bolstering their requirements for degrees and certification of new teachers, and these changes should be forcing educators in both schools of education and the disciplines to ask hard questions about their programs and teacher education in general. For example, when states mandate that all teachers graduate with a major in a discipline rather than in education, how should students who wish to become teachers be properly advised about the most appropriate major to pursue, especially if those students wish to teach in the primary grades? Should students who decide to teach at the high-school level pursue majors in a single discipline or a composite major? (The question arises in part because different states have developed different requirements about single vs. composite majors for certification at the secondary level.) How does the choice of a major affect the future teacher's professional options following graduation or five years hence? What

---

[2]Content standards for science and mathematics for every state that has developed them are available through "Achieve" (National Governors Conference) at <http://www.achieve.com>.

should the role of education programs be in states that mandate that all new teachers graduate with a major in something other than education? Given these changing regulations, how can a prospective teacher's preparation in education be tied more closely to that student's preparation in one or more disciplines, and vice versa?

Unfortunately, many faculty in science, mathematics, engineering, and technology (SME&T) at the nation's colleges and universities may not be sufficiently aware of these changing expectations to help prospective teachers learn and understand the content and concepts that are critical to effective teaching in these disciplines and their subject areas. Nor do most of these faculty have the kinds of professional development in teaching that would enable them to model effectively the kinds of pedagogy that is needed for success in grades K-12 classrooms (e.g., NRC, 1999h).

• **Accreditation standards for education programs may not reflect recent changes in expectations for classroom teaching.** For example, information technology will likely play an increasingly pervasive role in teaching and learning yet, according to several recent reports, teacher education programs are not providing prospective or practicing teachers with enough preparation to enable them to use information technology tools effectively to enhance teaching and learning (Milken Family Foundation, 1999; CEO Forum, 1999, 2000). While many educators and policy analysts consider educational technology as a vehicle for transforming education, relatively few teachers (20 percent) feel well equipped to institute technology integration in classroom instruction (U.S. Department of Education, 1999).[3]

• **Teacher licensing examinations do not always reflect recommended standards for teacher education or what states expect K-12 students to know or be able to do.** The content of teacher licensing examinations often does not reflect content espoused by such national standards documents as the *National Science Education Standards* (NRC, 1996a), the *Benchmarks for Science Literacy* (AAAS, 1993), and *Principles and Standards for School Mathematics* (NCTM, 2000). Nor do

---

[3]The International Society for Technology in Education released the National Educational Technology Standards and Performance Indicators for Teacher Education in June 2000. Sponsored by the U.S. Department of Education, these standards provide standards and benchmarks for "Essential Conditions for Teacher Preparation" and "Performance Profiles for Teacher Preparation" in the use of information technology at various stages of the teacher preparation process. Additional information about these standards is available at <http://cnets.iste.org/teachstand.html>.

they necessarily reflect state standards based in whole or in part on these national standards. In addition, teacher licensing examinations typically do not assess whether prospective teachers have become adept at planning and implementing the kinds of active pedagogies (e.g., inquiry, discourse) called for in national as well as some state science and mathematics standards.

• **Current rewards, incentives, and school environments are not adequate to attract large numbers of the best students to teaching or to encourage them to remain in the profession beyond the first few years of teaching.** These problems are exacerbated in science and mathematics, where teacher shortages already exist in many parts of the United States and are expected to grow worse over the next decade. The lack of teachers with adequate content knowledge and pedagogical skills for teaching science and mathematics is especially acute in small rural and inner city schools, where science or mathematics departments may consist of only one or two individuals and a given teacher may be required to teach several different subject areas every day (U.S. Department of Education, 1997a; Asimov, 1999; Shields et al., 1999; Public Agenda, 2000).

• **Professional development for continuing teachers (inservice education) too often consists of a patchwork of courses, curricula, and programs and may do little to enhance teachers' content knowledge or the techniques and skills they need to teach science and mathematics effectively.** The quality, coherence, and usefulness of professional development programs for improving the quality of teaching and student learning vary considerably. While all states mandate a minimum level of preparation in content and pedagogy for preservice teachers, there are few specific requirements for inservice education. In most states, the regulations that do exist for inservice education mandate only that teachers obtain some number of post-baccalaureate credits or a master's degree within some period of time after being hired and then to earn additional credits every few years thereafter. Content areas typically are not specified.

• **Against increasing expectations for performance, teachers are not sufficiently supported in professional development. In addition, they often have to undertake additional professional development on their own time and at their own expense.** Expectations for professional competence, performance, and accountability for teachers are increasing. These higher expectations are exemplified by the standards set forth by the

National Board for Professional Teaching Standards (NBPTS, 1994), the Interstate New Teacher Support Consortium (INTASC, 1999), and more strident calls by local, state, and national officials for more rigorous teacher education programs and licensing examinations. In addition, an increasing number of states have implemented (or will do so in the next several years) statewide testing programs for students, many of which place a strong emphasis on content knowledge. Because many of these tests will determine whether students can advance to higher grades or can earn high-school diplomas, teachers are under increasing pressure to become better versed in the content of the subject areas that they teach.

However, many school districts have not recognized nor responded to their responsibility to help teachers become better versed in their profession through well-planned, ongoing professional development programs. Inservice training within schools, where "one-size-fits-all" programs may be offered to teachers during the several professional development days during the school year, may not provide the knowledge teachers need to improve their ability to help students learn specific subjects such as science and mathematics. Inservice education for teachers also is among the first programs to be cut by school districts when resources are scarce or when school days are lost because of inclement weather or other unforeseen circumstances.

This lack of support for or provision of high-quality, professional development opportunities by school districts also is becoming increasingly coupled with demands by states that teachers acquire advanced degrees to become permanently certified. As a result, teachers often must continue their education and professional development on their own time and, unlike many other professions, at their own expense.

Policy Position:

- *Teachers are committed to students and their learning.*
- *Teachers know the subjects they teach and how to teach those subjects to students.*
- *Teachers are responsible for managing and monitoring student learning.*
- *Teachers think systematically about their practice and learn from experience.*
- *Teachers are members of learning communities.*

National Board for Professional Teaching Standards, 1994

THE TEACHING PROFESSION

As summarized below, many other professions have developed and adopted coherent, well-recognized procedures and policies for attracting, educating, and inducting new members to the profession. Many of these other professions also have well-understood and accepted expectations for high-quality performance by practitioners, the expectation that practitioners will upgrade their knowledge and skills throughout their careers, and an enabling continuing education system. Often these types of standards are developed and maintained by the members of the profession through accrediting boards and the professional societies that represent them. People who meet or exceed those professional expectations typically are rewarded and recognized in ways that are both tangible and appropriate.

The National Board for Professional Teaching Standards (1994) has articulated such standards or guidelines for the teaching profession. That these guidelines are available but have been widely overlooked or ignored by the nation's education system is a symptom of a lack of attention to the professional needs of teachers. This lack of attention to teachers as professionals betrays a certain lack of respectful treatment that permeates the continuum of the careers of teachers in the following ways:

• **Career Advising:** Colleges and universities routinely assign an individual or empanel a committee to attend to the needs of students who are preparing for other professions (e.g., medicine, law, or engineering). In contrast, science and mathematics departments rarely have people who are sufficiently knowledgeable about K-12 teaching in the sciences or mathematics to offer students the guidance they need. Many college faculty in science, mathematics, and engineering who serve as academic advisors actually know very little about career opportunities in K-12 teaching or the requirements for entering the profession and may offer very little encouragement to students to pursue a career in teaching.

• **Rigor and appropriateness of content courses for prospective teachers:** Perception can govern action, whether those perceptions are accurate or not. In some institutions, both faculty and students may perceive that courses in science and mathematics designed for teachers are less rigorous or challenging than courses designed for students who are preparing for most other professions (e.g., introductory physics or calculus for pre-engineering students) (see also NRC, 1997b, Lewis and Tucker, in press).

• **Oversight of teacher education programs by professional organizations:** Unlike the requirements and standards that they establish for students who wish to pursue more traditional careers in a discipline, many disciplinary professional organizations do not claim "ownership" of teacher preparation programs for that discipline. Indeed, many college-level faculty in the sciences, mathematics, engineering, or technology are unaware of expectations for content or even the existence of state or national standards for teacher preparation in their own disciplines. This lack of common expectations can result in teachers with similar degrees having experienced substantially different levels of preparation during their preservice years.

• **The continuum of professional development:** Other professions mark the awarding of the baccalaureate degree as the beginning of a career path. Focused and directed professional growth is expected and supported in the ensuing years. For example, no doctor is considered to have received sufficient education upon the awarding of the medical degree to practice a specialty. Intensive residencies and fellowships that involve extensive additional education, mentoring, and direct work with acknowledged experts in the field are routinely expected. Following licensing in a specialty, regular upgrading of skills and knowledge within the specialty and related fields is required. In contrast, college graduates who enter teaching

often are viewed as being ready to assume full duties in the classroom and too often are assigned the most challenging teaching responsibilities in their schools. Many beginning teachers in the United States cite the lack of guidance, time for preparation and reflection, and opportunities to grow in the profession as primary frustrations of teaching (Hoff, 2000; NSTA, 2000).

As with other professions, teachers must master a rapidly changing body of knowledge, serve a constantly changing clientele, and deal with the pressure of new societal expectations. For professions deemed critical to the well being of society (e.g., biomedical research and clinical practice), private and governmental agencies and organizations often expand funding to accommodate such changes and retrain practitioners. In contrast, K-12 education—although critical to the well-being of individuals, communities, and society at large—does not receive similar support, especially at the state and local levels where it is controlled and operated.

• **Mentoring of new employees:** Neophytes in many other professions (and teachers in other nations) are routinely placed under the tutelage and guidance of more experienced teachers—mentors—for extended periods of time. Novices may be assigned fewer specific work responsibilities during the early parts of their careers so they can both learn more about their disciplines and become reflective about the practice of their professions. Mentoring of novice teachers in the United States has been haphazard at best (Education Trust, 1998; Darling-Hammond and Macdonald, 2000), although a new study by the Urban Teacher Collaborative[4] (Haselkorn and Harris, 1998; Fideler and Haselkorn, 1999; Urban Teacher Collaborative, 2000) shows that mentoring has been successful in some large urban areas. While some districts and states pay close attention to the first few years of teachers' careers, most do not.

• **Targeted professional development programs:** Professional development programs in most professions are directed toward providing practitioners with information and resources that are appropriate for their specific job responsibilities and career levels. Because employers assume that entry-level employees do *not* yet possess the high-level skills and insights of more senior colleagues, professional development is geared toward the acquisition of increasingly sophisticated lifelong professional skills, perspectives, and learning. Mentors are often useful in helping with this process. In teaching, however, many of the more abstract ideas (e.g.,

education and learning theory) may be presented before practitioners ever set foot in a classroom. Inservice programs, in turn, may offer more experienced teachers information and perspectives about teaching that might be better suited to preservice students or those who are about to begin their teaching careers.

• **Encouragement and incentives for continuing education within the profession:** Employers who require or encourage people in the early stages of their careers to pursue additional education either pay completely for or subsidize the costs of such advanced training. In turn, it is expected that the employees' additional education will enhance the skills they need in their current positions and prepare them for new opportunities within the company and profession. Although many school districts now require teachers to complete master's degrees or continuing education units to obtain lifetime certification, there are few requirements or expectations that teachers will pursue those advanced degrees in the subject areas in which they actually instruct.

• **Expectations for credentialing of professionals:** Statistics indicate that people are changing careers more frequently now than ever before (synthe-

---

[4]The Urban Teacher Collaborative is a joint initiative sponsored by Recruiting New Teachers, Inc. (<http://www.rnt.org/>), The Council of the Great City Schools (<http://www.cgcs.org>), and The Council of the Great City Colleges of Education (<http://www.cgcs.org/services/Cgcce/index.html>).

sized in NRC, 1999b). People moving into professional schools or professions through nontraditional routes generally expect to take prerequisite and required courses first. And they do so because the financial and other rewards they expect, eventually, make the investment of time and money worthwhile. However, financial compensation and other rewards are much less for teachers than for other professionals.[5] Therefore, those who might consider becoming teachers after experience in other professions have few incentives to spend the several years and the money required to take education or subject-matter courses for teacher certification (U.S. Department of Education, 1999; AFT, 2000). Under these conditions, a variety of alternative paths to certification have evolved.[6] There has been much debate about both the efficacy of many of these alternative certification programs (e.g., Feistritzer and Chester, 2000; AFT, 2000) and the financial

incentives that districts have to hire these individuals rather than teachers with more professional experience.

• **Involvement of employees in decision- and policy-making:** Experience in modern business and industry has pointed to the critical importance of workers at all levels being included in workplace and product design, planning, and decision-making (e.g., Murnane and Levy, 1997; Rust, 1998). Workers who have spent many years assembling products have been found often to be the best people to provide advice to management about ways to increase productivity and efficiency in an industry. And, in turn, workers are being rewarded for this.

However, these kinds of changes in the workplace have not yet reached much of K-12 education. In many school districts, classroom teachers still do not have the authority or power to effect meaningful change in what they do, how they do it, or the environments

---

[5]According to the National Center for Education Statistics' *Digest of Education Statistics* (1999 ed.), the average salary for all teachers across the U.S. in 1997-1998 was $39,385, and since 1990-1991, salaries for teachers have actually fallen slightly after being adjusted for inflation.

[6]The term, "alternative certification," encompasses a very wide set of philosophies and approaches to allowing people to become teachers. Feistritzer and Chester (2000) state "…'alternative certification' has been used to refer to every avenue to becoming licensed to teach, from emergency certification to very sophisticated and well-designed programs that address the professional preparation needs of the growing population of individuals who already have at least a baccalaureate degree and considerable life experience and want to become teachers." Feistritzer and Chester also point out that nearly all states now offer opportunities to people who have earned college degrees in fields other than education to return to college, major in education, and become certified teachers. Several states provide alternative routes to teaching where individuals with bachelor's degrees can engage in "on-the-job training" while taking various college level courses (vs. a full-time program). However, many more states are now looking into authorizing other types of alternative pathways to certification.

in which they work. For example, the curricular materials that teachers are expected to use are typically either selected by committees with members drawn from diverse constituencies or mandated by the district or state. Most K-12 teachers also do not have work-spaces separate from their students or even access to a telephone within their workspace for work-related communications. Exceptional enterprise or innovation may not be tangibly rewarded due to workplace rules.[7] Senior teachers typically are not asked to offer their expertise, insights, and perspectives to help improve teacher education programs for less senior colleagues.

In addition, data from TIMSS (e.g., Stigler and Hiebert, 1997) and evaluation of new approaches to teacher education (e.g., see Chapter 4 and examples in Appendixes D and E, such as UTeach at the University of Texas) indicate that, in addition to providing input to the operations of their schools and districts, teachers also need time and flexibility in their schedules to build a "teaching community" where they can actively and openly discuss content and pedagogy. As discussed by Ball (1997), this teaching community also is a place where teachers can offer constructive

criticism and support to help each other improve their teaching.

• **Clientele and professional working conditions:** U.S. schools and teachers are facing challenges today that were largely unimagined and unanticipated even 30 years ago. The education system in the United States now works with a more diverse student population than ever before. Teachers in both large metropolitan areas and more rural locales must try to educate the children of large and varied populations of immigrants, many of whom arrive at school unable to speak English. Some of these children—as well as their parents—have received little or no formal education even in their first languages before arriving in the United States. In addition, teachers are working with more types of "special needs" students, including those who are physically challenged or developmentally or emotionally delayed, than ever before. Teachers also are working increasingly with some students who come from families that offer them little stability or support at home. For teachers of science and mathematics, this latter problem can be exacerbated by the fact that some parents from all walks of life are not sufficiently familiar or comfort-

---

[7]Some districts and states are reconsidering their policies about additional financial incentives for teachers. For example, the National Conference of State Legislatures reported that, in 1999, 15 state legislatures had proposed or established incentives that encourage and reward teachers' knowledge and skills (Hirsch, 2000).

able with the content and approaches to teaching the subjects in these disciplines to be able to help or encourage their children.

Unlike the facilities and resources that are routinely provided to people in other professions, the facilities and equipment provided to teachers in schools are often dilapidated or outdated (Lewis et al., 2000). Many science laboratories may not conform to current codes for safety, and most were not built to facilitate teaching and learning of science as articulated in national standards (Biehle et al., 1999). Science equipment may be obsolete or in need of routine repair or calibration. There is little technical support to maintain equipment or resolve technical problems that teachers or students encounter. In those cases where concerted efforts have been made to outfit schools with modern equipment (e.g., desktop computers connected to the Internet), teachers may not receive the preservice preparation or ongoing professional training needed to use this equipment in ways that truly enhance student learning and achievement (Knuth et al., 1996; Valdez et al. 1999; Downes, 2000).

As a result of these conditions, many teachers are becoming both disenchanted with and disenfranchised from their profession. For example, a recent survey by the National Science Teachers Association (NSTA) has concluded that nearly 40 percent of science teachers in the United States are considering leaving their jobs. The primary reason cited was job dissatisfaction stemming largely from low pay and lack of support from principals (*Education Week,* 2000). A report from the Texas State Teachers Association reported similar levels of dissatisfaction among teachers in that state (Henderson, 2000).

These conditions also may be influencing the career choices of young people. In 1999, a survey of 501 college-bound high-school students from Montgomery County, MD, public schools indicated that a majority of these students was reluctant even to consider teaching as a career option. Reporting out the results from the survey, Hart Research Associates (1999)[8] stated that 39 percent of the students in the survey had no interest in becoming teachers in public schools, with another 16 percent expressing little interest. Participants in two focus groups also reported out by Hart Research Associates (one of boys, one of girls) concentrated their remarks on the poor image of teachers and the public's general lack of respect for the

---

[8]Additional information about the methods and results of this survey is available at <http://www.mff.org/newsroom>.

teaching profession. Although 55 percent of the respondents would at least consider careers as teachers, some are likely to lose interest in teaching as they proceed through college, particularly if they are interested enough in science, mathematics, or engineering to declare a major in one of these disciplines (Seymour and Hewitt, 1997). Further, the feedback given by the focus groups about their images of teachers and teaching was revealing. Students in the focus group recognized that, "for their entire careers, teachers remain at the level at which they began unless they decide to go into the administrative side of education. There is no higher position for which to strive, no room for promotion, and little opportunity for significant salary increases." Hart Associates concluded, "While the polling results indicate that young people have little interest in being teachers, the focus group sessions—in which we hear the actual 'voices' of college-bound students—are especially sobering. Simply put, we are dealing with a generation of youth whose values, outlook, and career goals seemingly run counter to what it takes to be interested in teaching. On the one hand, most of these students profess admiration for the teaching profession; they understand that shaping young minds is important work. On the other hand, they view the job of being a teacher as work that is uninteresting."

Thus, the Committee on Science and Mathematics Teacher Preparation is convinced that the *status quo* in the education and professional development of teachers of science and mathematics does not meet the needs of either teachers or the teaching profession. Most importantly, current approaches to the various phases of teacher education do not and will not serve the needs of the nation's students in the next decade and beyond. As many recent reports already have stated, improving teacher education and the treatment of teachers as professionals in science, mathematics, and technology will require the cooperation and collaboration of a multitude of disparate institutions, agencies, and organizations, many of which have had minimal contact with each other and few incentives to work together. If the United States genuinely values high-quality education for its children, its leaders and decision-makers should not allow the present state of affairs to persist.

Further, the committee's reviews of the research data and of other reports and recommendations have led the members to conclude that teaching must involve continual professional development, growth, and progressive leadership responsibilities for teachers over the span of their careers. The committee's vision of teacher education, as articulated in this report, is one that involves a complex, multidimensional, and career-long process. This vision (detailed in Chapter 6) emphasizes the intellectual growth and maturation of teachers of science and mathematics and increasing the professionalism of teaching in these disciplines and in general. The vision would be achieved through genuine partnerships that exhibit the following characteristics:

• They would be developed and implemented collaboratively by scientists, mathematicians, engineers; science, mathematics, and technology educators; and teachers of grades K-12.

• *All* colleges and universities, whether or not they offer formal teacher education programs, would make teacher education one of their institution's central priorities.[9] The highest levels of leadership from postsecondary education communities would affirm their institutions' commitment to teacher education as a basic tenet of their educational mission. Higher education

organizations would assist their member institutions to develop programs to increase awareness of *all* faculty members about the importance of teacher education and their roles in it.

• Each postsecondary institution would establish clear connections between its programs and professional consensus about what beginning and more experienced teachers should know and be able to do in their classrooms.[10] Teacher education programs would meet the highest standards that have been articulated by national professional organizations.

• Institutions of higher education would maintain contact with and provide guidance for teachers who complete their preparation and development programs after those teachers leave the campus. Higher education organizations would assist higher education institution members in establishing programs for new teachers who have moved to the regions served by those institutions.

• Professional disciplinary societies in science, mathematics, and engineer-

---

[9]The nation's teacher workforce consists of many individuals who have matriculated at all types of two- and four-year colleges and universities. Although many of these schools do not offer formal teacher education programs, virtually every institution of higher education, through the kinds of courses it offers, the teaching it models, and the advising it provides to students, has the potential to influence whether or not its graduates will pursue careers in teaching.

[10]For example, the Interstate New Teacher Assessment and Support Consortium (INTASC) has developed consensus guidelines for preservice programs under the auspices of the Council of Chief State School Officers. Additional information about INTASC is available at <http://www.ccsso.org/intasc.html>. Corresponding consensus guidelines for continuing professional development have been developed by the National Board for Professional Teaching Standards (NBPTS). Additional information about NBPTS is available at <http://www.nbpts.org/nbpts/>.

ing, higher education organizations, governments at all levels, and the private sector would become more engaged partners in efforts to improve teacher education in science, mathematics, and technology. Professional disciplinary societies also would work together to align their own policies and recommendations on teacher education.

• Universities whose primary mission includes education research would set as a priority the development and execution of studies that focus on ways to improve teaching and learning for people of all ages (e.g., AAU Presidents' Resolution on Teacher Education, 1999; NRC, 1999f). Government agencies would also set this priority. New research

that focuses broadly on synthesizing data across studies and linking it to school practice in a wide variety of school settings would be especially helpful to the improvement of teacher education and professional development for both prospective and experienced teachers.

• Concomitant with such collaboration would be the development of a culture of education that recognizes all of these partners as having equal voices at the table. All partners would be equally responsible for the leadership required to prepare future educators and improve the knowledge base and skills of *all* practicing teachers in both the K-12 and higher education sectors.

3
The Critical Importance of Well-Prepared Teachers for Student Learning and Achievement

Nearly everyone now accepts the premise that teachers make a difference in the lives of their students. One report (Coleman et al., 1966) briefly cast doubt on the direct importance of teachers in student achievement. This report seemed to indicate that the impact of teachers and the quality of teaching were less important to student learning and achievement than other factors, such as students' socioeconomic status. However, subsequent research in classrooms has demonstrated that teachers do make a tangible difference in student achievement. For example, variation in student achievement has been systematically related to variation in the classroom behaviors of teachers (as summarized in a review of the literature by Good et al., 1975).

Reflecting these findings, King and Newman (2000) state, "Since teachers have the most direct, sustained contact with students and considerable control over what is taught and the climate for learning, improving teachers' knowledge, skills and dispositions through professional development is a critical step in improving student achievement." The National Commission on Teaching and America's Future (NCTAF, 1996) and other national groups, such as the Education Trust (1998), earlier reached similar conclusions based on research that tracked the academic achievement of individual students over long time periods (see, for example, Sanders and Rivers, 1996). Further, all of these organizations have shown that well-qualified teachers and high-quality teaching can close the achievement gap between economically disadvantaged students and their more affluent peers.

The public also recognizes the importance of well-prepared teachers. In a large survey, Haselkorn and Harris (1998) reported that "roughly nine out of ten Americans believe the best way to

Public opinion overwhelmingly favors "ensuring a well-qualified teacher in every classroom" as the top education priority. Indeed, teachers—once viewed as central to the problem of student underachievement—are now being recognized as the solution. In teacher preparation there is a "multiplier effect" that can span generations. While a sound undergraduate science education is essential for producing the next generation of scientists, it is equally critical for future teachers of science. The refrain, "You can't teach what you don't know," surely applies.

National Science Board, 1999

lift student achievement is to ensure a qualified teacher in every classroom." This survey revealed, in addition, a strong belief by the public that prospective teachers need special training and skills, not simply a good general education.

It is important to examine the veracity of the conclusion that well-prepared teachers and high-quality teaching matter. It also is important to document and understand what specific characteristics of teachers, and the school settings in which they work, contribute to successful student outcomes. This

information can then be used to help determine how better to educate and support successful teachers. If high-quality teaching is essential to success in student learning and if the academic success and achievement of students can be linked to specific characteristics of teaching—such information might be used to argue against a recent trend in many districts toward dilution of requirements for teacher education and certification in response to teacher shortages, class-size reductions, and growing K-12 student populations.

Figure 3-1 provides an overview of how research data, recommendations of professional organizations and their reports, national standards for teachers of science and mathematics, and extant standards for K-12 students in science and mathematics can influence the quality of K-12 teachers, teaching, and student achievement.

THE EVIDENCE THAT HIGH-QUALITY TEACHING MATTERS

Before discussing further the various aspects of teacher quality, the study committee wishes to acknowledge and to emphasize that there are countless thousands of science and mathematics teachers who do excellent jobs in helping their students learn and achieve, often in very difficult circumstances and at

FIGURE 3-1 Factors that influence teacher quality and quality teaching and their effects on student achievement. Depicted are four areas examined in this report and describing what is known about preparing quality teachers and their impact on K-12 student achievement in mathematics and science.

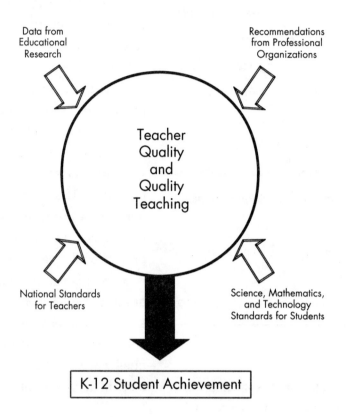

relatively low pay. The committee's list of concerns and recommendations for addressing those concerns are not intended to paint all teachers with the same brush. Indeed, most of the concerns expressed in this report can be attributed to preparation and continuing professional development that are now either out-of-date or inadequate to meet the demands of new approaches to teaching and learning of science and mathematics. However, everyone who is concerned about the quality of education should consider carefully adopting policies and practices that encourage the most qualified individuals to prepare for, enter, and remain in science and mathematics teaching and revamping or jettisoning those practices that dissuade or impede them from doing so.

In the last few years, a number of large-scale studies of teaching have elucidated how teacher quality makes a difference in the achievement of students. Three of these studies and their conclusions are summarized below. An examination of studies that focus more specifically on science and mathematics teaching and K-12 student achievement follows.

TEACHER QUALITY AND GENERAL STUDENT ACHIEVEMENT: THREE STUDIES

Later reports frequently cite studies by Sanders and colleagues (see below), Ferguson (1991), and Ferguson and Ladd (1996) as evidence that the qualifications of teachers not only matter in student achievement but also are major variables in improving student learning and achievement.

For over 15 years, Sanders and his colleagues associated with the Tennessee Value-Added Assessment System (TVAAS) have analyzed data from annual tests in mathematics, science, reading, language, and social studies given to grade 3-8 students in Tennessee. Utilizing a database now in excess of 5 million records, Sanders and his colleagues have tracked individual students over time and studied each child's academic achievement year by year. In this way, they have been able to identify a year when a child makes average progress, exceeds average progress, or achieves no gain.

In a study intended to gauge the cumulative and residual effects of teacher qualifications on student achievement, Sanders and Rivers (1996) gathered test or achievement data for a cohort of students from the time they were second-graders to the time they had completed fifth grade. By disaggregating the data, the researchers were able to see the impact of quality teaching on each child over time (Sanders and Rivers, 1996).[1] Sanders and Rivers reported that student achievement at each grade level correlated positively with the quality of the teachers who taught those students. Also of interest was the researchers' discovery of residual effects; that is, they found that the individual children they studied tended not to recover after a school

---

[1]Sanders, Rivers, and their colleagues did not define teacher quality *a priori*. Rather they sought to identify "quality" teachers based on how well students achieved in one year of school. Using the Tennessee achievement tests as a measure, they determined if the students in a given teacher's class achieved a normal year of growth in various subject matter fields such as mathematics or more or less than a normal year's academic growth. Using these criteria, they then identified teachers as "below average quality," "average quality," or "above average quality."

year's worth of classroom experience with an ineffective teacher. Conversely, a child who spent one year with a highly effective teacher tended to experience academic benefits even two years later. In this and other studies, Sanders and his colleagues have shown that placing students in classrooms with high-quality teaching does matter. Variables such as the racial and/or ethnic composition of schools, students' socioeconomic levels, and the mean achievement of an entire school correlated far less with student achievement when compared to the variable of teacher quality.

In a large-scale study of younger children in grades 3-5, Sanders and colleagues Wright and Horn found that "teacher effects are dominant factors affecting student academic gain," especially in mathematics but also, noticeably, in science (Wright et al., 1997).

In a 1991 study, Ferguson examined student scores on standardized tests in reading and mathematics, teacher qualifications, and class size in 900 out of 1,000 school districts in Texas. The teacher qualifications examined in each district included teacher performance on the Texas state teacher examinations, years of teaching experience, and teachers' acquisition of advanced (master's) degrees. Ferguson (1991) found that the following teacher qualifications, listed in order from most to least important, had statistically signifi-

cant effects on student scores: teacher language scores on the state examination, class size, years of teaching experience, and the earning of an advanced degree. According to a review of the study conducted by the National Center for Education Statistics (cited in Sparks and Hirsh, 2000), teacher expertise, as Ferguson had defined it, explained 40 percent of the variance in the students' achievement in reading and mathematics.

Later, in 1996, Ferguson and Ladd used Sanders' statistical approach to study nearly 30,000 Alabama fourth graders during the 1990-91 school year. They found that students' test scores in mathematics and reading were positively affected by two teacher variables: higher than average scores on the American College Testing program's college entrance examination and completion of one or more master's degrees.

Since teachers have the most direct, sustained contact with students and considerable control over what is taught and the climate for learning, improving teachers' knowledge, skill and dispositions through professional development is a critical step in improving student achievement.

King and Newman, 2000

TEACHER QUALITY AND STUDENT ACHIEVEMENT IN SCIENCE AND MATHEMATICS

Research that attempted to investigate the relationship between teacher quality and student achievement began in earnest in the 1960s and 1970s. In a meta-analysis of previous work, Druva and Anderson (1983) uncovered a number of important and statistically significant positive correlations that shed light on the variable of teacher quality in science instruction. Teaching background, teacher behavior in the classroom, and student outcomes were examined. Findings included that teachers with greater content knowledge in a given subject and those with more teaching experience were more likely to ask higher level, cognitively based questions. Teachers with more content knowledge also had a greater orientation toward seeking information from students through questioning and discussion in their teaching compared to teachers with less content knowledge. This was particularly significant in the case of biology teachers. Students' ability to understand the essentials of the scientific method was positively correlated with the number of science courses (both in biology and in other science disciplines) that their teachers had taken. The degree to which students reported that they "liked science" correlated positively with the number of science courses taken by the teachers.

In 1989, McDiarmid et al. concluded, on the basis of research extant at the time, that teachers' subject matter understanding and their pedagogical orientations and decisions critically influence the quality of their teaching. "Teachers' capacity to pose questions, select tasks, evaluate their pupil's understanding, and to make curricular decisions all depend on how they themselves understand the subject matter." And in 1995, Chaney demonstrated a relationship between middle-school science and mathematics teachers' professional preparation and student performance.

These consistently positive correlations appear to support the importance of high levels of preparation for teachers in both content and pedagogy. This preparation and subsequent teaching experience also appear to enhance student achievement.

THE IMPORTANCE OF TEACHER CERTIFICATION

Hawk et al. (1985) conducted a specific study of the relationship between teachers' certification in mathematics and their teaching effectiveness. Two groups, each of 18 teachers who had taught at least one course in mathematics in grades 6-12, participated in the seven-month study. One group consisted of teachers who held either subject area certification or endorsement in mathematics ("in-field teachers"), and the other group consisted of teachers who lacked these credentials ("out-of-field teachers"). Both groups of teachers taught the same mathematics course in the same school to students of the same general ability. Pretest scores of students across the different groups did not differ significantly from each other. Researchers proceeded to examine comparative teacher effectiveness by looking at student achievement,[2] teacher professional skills,[3] and teacher knowledge of the subject field.[4]

Students taught by in-field teachers scored significantly higher on general mathematics (p< .001) and algebra (p<.01) tests than did students taught by out-of-field teachers. In-field teachers scored significantly higher (p<.001) on the test of teachers' subject matter knowledge than did out-of-field teachers. In-field teachers also scored significantly higher (p<. 001) on the *Carolina Teacher Performance Assessment System* than did their out-of-field counterparts. No significant differences were observed between the two groups based on years of teaching experience, years of experience teaching mathematics, or level of degree earned. Overall, in-field mathematics teachers knew more mathematics and showed evidence of using more effective teaching practices than did their out-of-field counterparts. Hawk et al. (1985) concluded that certification requirements are an effective mechanism to assure higher student achievement in mathematics.

Also important to this discussion are Ingersoll's (1999) findings that, nationwide, approximately one third of all secondary school teachers of mathematics have neither a major nor a minor in mathematics, mathematics education, or in such related disciplines as engineering or physics. Similarly, about 20 percent of science teachers lack even a minor in science or science education, and "over half of teachers teaching physical sciences classes (chemistry,

---

[2]Student achievement was measured with the *Stanford Achievement Test* (general mathematics) and the *Stanford Test of Academic Skills* (algebra).

[3]Teacher professional skills were observed for an entire class period twice during the seven-month period by trained observers who used the *Carolina Teacher Performance Assessment System* (CTPAS). This instrument focuses on five teaching characteristics: management of instructional time, management of student behavior, instructional presentation, instructional monitoring, and instructional feedback. The inter-rater reliability exceeded 90 percent.

[4]*Descriptive Tests of Mathematics Skills* (arithmetic and elementary algebra skills) were used to measure teachers' subject matter knowledge.

physics, earth science, or space science) are without an academic major or minor in any one of the physical sciences" (Ingersoll, 1999).[5,6] As one might expect, the situation was worse in high-poverty schools. The fact that significant numbers of the more than 314,000 current secondary school science and mathematics teachers are teaching without full certification in these subjects should cause significant concern about the science and mathematics instruction children may or may not be receiving.

These concerns are reinforced by Fetler (1999), who investigated the relationship between measures of a teacher's experience with mathematics and educational level and student achievement in mathematics. Fetler used scores from the administration of the *Stanford Achievement Test* (*Stanford 9*) to 1.3 million students in grades 9 through 11 in 785 California high schools. The test's content is oriented toward basic skills and its publisher claims that it is based on NCTM standards in mathematics (NCTM, 1989). Fetler found that three variables related to teacher preparation correlated with student test scores: the number of teachers in those high schools with emergency teaching permits, teaching experience as measured by years of service (excluding substitute experience), and teachers' educational level. Specifically, (1) student test results correlated positively with amount of teaching experience, (2) lower average student test scores in a school corre-

---

[5]For high-school physics teachers, Ingersoll's data are corroborated by a recent report from the American Institute of Physics (Neuschatz and McFarling, 1999). However, Neuschatz and McFarling were optimistic about what they reviewed as an improving situation in the teaching of physics: "Contrary to widely-circulating reports, the preparation of high-school physics teachers seems to be generally, albeit slowly, improving, and cases of instructors with no physics background are rare. A third have degrees in physics or physics education, and if those with physics minors are included, the proportion approaches one-half... Virtually all the rest have a degree in mathematics or another science, or in math or science education. In the past, we have found that more than 80% had taken three or more college physics courses." (Neuschatz and McFarling, 1999). Further, the number of people teaching physics with bachelors degrees in that discipline has increased during the 1990s: from 24 percent in 1990 to 29 percent in 1993 to 43 percent in 1997 (Neuschatz and McFarling, 1999).

[6]Survey data collected by Neuschatz and McFarling (1999) also suggest that, at least for physics teachers, time spent teaching the subject also might influence the quality of teaching, irrespective of formal academic credentials in the discipline. Many teachers without formal credentials in physics who were surveyed in 1993 had reported that they felt ill prepared to teach the subject. When surveyed again in 1997, many of these same teachers saw themselves as adequately- or well-prepared to teach physics and attributed the change to the experience they had gained from actually preparing for and presenting the course, laboratories, and demonstrations. Neuschatz and McFarling (1999) emphasized, however, that definitive data are not yet available to determine whether the students of these experienced teachers without formal preparation in the discipline fare as well on physics examinations as students whose teachers have acquired formal credentials in physics.

lated with higher numbers of teachers with emergency permits in that school, and (3) higher average student scores in a school correlated higher levels of education among the teachers in that school. After controlling for socioeconomic status, Fetler concluded that student achievement in mathematics significantly correlated with teacher experience and preparation.

As a result of his study, Fetler (1999), commented, "After controlling for poverty, teacher experience and preparation significantly predict test scores" and "Schools with higher percentages of teachers on emergency permits tended to have lower achieving students in mathematics."

In light of the positive impact of in-field teaching on student achievement, why is out-of-field teaching so prevalent and what might be done to curtail the practice? This report examines that issue more fully in a subsequent section on recruiting teachers and staffing schools (see Chapter 6 "Other Benefits of Partnerships for Teacher Education in Science and Mathematics").

DATA FROM NATIONAL AND INTERNATIONAL TESTS

Studies of the National Assessment of Educational Progress (NAEP)[7] also point to the importance of teachers' levels of content preparation. Although the NAEP is designed primarily to determine how U.S. students are doing in various subjects at grades 4, 8, and 12, recent NAEPs also have collected some data about the teachers whose students took these examinations (e.g., Hawkins et al., 1998). The 1996 data show a statistically significant correlation coefficient of 0.26 between the percentage of students whose teachers have a college major in mathematics and the average mathematics scores of those students (Hawkins et al., 1998). Hence, there is some evidence to suggest the position that the more well versed a teacher is in the subject, the better his/her students do on this type of standardized examination. Hawkins et al. (1998) concluded that, "At the eighth-grade level, students who were taught by teachers with teaching certificates in mathematics outperformed students

---

[7]The National Assessment of Educational Progress (NAEP) conducts assessments of samples of the nation's students attending public and private schools at the elementary-, junior-, and high-school levels. NAEP collects and reports information about the academic performance of American students in a wide variety of learning areas, including subjects such as reading, math, science, writing, world and U.S. history, civics, and foreign languages. NAEP uses a complex matrix sampling design in order to cover a broad array of topics. The design allows for reporting of aggregated results for various population groups, but no individual results are reported.

whose teachers had teaching certificates in education or an 'other' field."

The Third International Mathematics and Science Study (TIMSS) collected information in the mid-1990s on student performance in these subjects around the world and also gathered information about teachers. In mathematics, fourth-grade students in the United States scored slightly above average on the TIMSS examination, but eighth- and twelfth-grade students performed below and well below average, respectively. The findings from the science component of TIMSS indicate that fourth and eighth graders scored above the international average in science. However, U.S. twelfth graders performed below the international average in science, and the United States ranked among the lowest of 21 nations in the TIMSS end-of-secondary school assessment of science general knowledge. Overall, the "international standing of U.S. students was stronger at the eighth-grade level than at the twelfth-grade level in both mathematics and science among the countries that participated in the assessments at both grade levels"

(U.S. Department of Education, 1997b; Harmon et al., 1997). These findings suggest that a study of the characteristics of teachers in U.S. middle schools might possibly point to ways to change teacher preparation in mathematics (National Science Board, 1999; NRC, 1999c).

Another component of TIMSS with direct bearing on issues in mathematics teacher preparation is Stigler and Hiebert's (1997) comparative analysis of TIMSS videotapes of grade 8 mathematics classes in Germany, Japan, and the United States.[8] The comparison shows some startling differences in the instructional practices of mathematics teachers among the three countries (U. S. Department of Education, 1996; NRC, 1999c), such as

- Japanese teachers widely practice what the U.S. mathematics reform effort has recommended, while U.S. teachers do so less frequently.

- An emphasis on cultivating student understanding is evident in the steps typical of Japanese grade 8 mathematics lessons. In contrast, an emphasis on skill acquisition is evident in the steps

---

[8]Between 50 and 100 eighth-grade classes in mathematics were videotaped in each country. The tapes were then digitized, transcribed, and translated into English. Expert evaluators coded the videotapes for the occurrence of specific content elements and teaching and curricular events and then analyzed the data quantitatively. Teachers whose classes were videotaped also completed questionnaires about what they were planning to teach during the sessions so that teacher intentions and actual events could be compared. For more details, see Stigler and Hiebert (1997) and National Research Council (1999c). Similar video recordings are now being prepared that will examine science teaching in eighth-grade classrooms in different countries. These videos should be available late in 2001.

common to most U.S. and German mathematics lessons.

- The U.S. and German emphasis on skills rather than understanding also carries over into the type of mathematics work that students are assigned to do at their desks during class.
- U.S. teachers rarely develop mathematical concepts, in contrast to German and Japanese teachers.

It is important to recognize that directly relating the NAEP and TIMSS data about teacher training or practices and approaches to student performance is difficult at best. For example, more experienced teachers with better mathematics backgrounds may be assigned to teach classes composed of more motivated or more well-prepared students (U.S. Department of Education, 1996). It also is important to understand that student performance on these kinds of standardized examinations reflects the curriculum studied up to the time students take a particular examination, a state or a nation's cultural emphasis on and support for education, and many other variables. Some of these factors are likely to have at least as much influence on test performance, if not more so, than teachers. Despite these other interact-

ing variables, however, it is revealing that nearly 40 percent of grade 8 students in the United States learn mathematics from teachers who do not have college majors in either mathematics or mathematics education (Hawkins et al., 1998).

Nonetheless, in terms of certification, many eighth-grade teachers have sufficient backgrounds in mathematics to be certified in mathematics in many states. For example, 15 units in mathematics (with some specified variety of courses) were cited as satisfactory preparation for junior high-school mathematics teachers in the last recommendations of the Mathematical Association of America (1991)[9] (although some states do require additional units in the subject). Yet, the TIMSS videos and test results suggest that even those teachers with certification in the discipline are teaching only a limited array of mathematical concepts and skills and doing so in ways that may be ineffective for long-term learning and mastery. The TIMSS video data also suggest that, unlike their counterparts in other countries such as Japan, many U.S. mathematics teachers present mathematical manipulations and algorithms to their students without first making certain that the students understand how and why such procedures are used.

---

[9]An updated version of these recommendations from the Conference Board on the Mathematical Sciences will call for 21 hours in mathematics for all middle-school mathematics teachers. Additional information is available at <http://www.maa.org/cbms/metdraft/index.htm>.

These differences in approach and emphasis may account for the lower performance of U.S. students on the kinds of questions that were asked on the TIMSS examination. It is telling that the eighth grade students whose teachers were most knowledgeable about the NCTM standards extant at that time performed better on the NAEP than did students whose teachers knew little or nothing about those standards (Hawkins et al., 1998).

Taken together, the TIMSS data on student achievement in mathematics and the NAEP data on teachers' mathematics backgrounds lend support to the proposition that students perform better when they are able to learn from teachers who know their subject matter well and who are well informed about improved ways to teach.

CONTENT PREPARATION IS CRITICAL FOR HIGH-QUALITY TEACHING IN SCIENCE AND MATHEMATICS

What level and type of subject-matter knowledge (content knowledge) do K-12 teachers of science or mathematics need? Teacher educators and subject matter specialists have been trying to address this question for many years. One straightforward answer comes from examining the national standards in science and mathematics for grades K-12. The national standards for K-12 science and mathematics do not dictate the level of knowledge required of K-12 teachers. Some find it reasonable to suggest, however, that, at a bare minimum, teachers should possess knowledge and deep understanding of the subject matter recommended for students at the level of their teaching and, preferably, one grade level category above their particular teaching level.[10] Thus, the science knowledge set forth in the *National Science Education Standards* for middle-level students would be the minimum level of science knowledge required of teachers for the elementary grades.[11] The mathematics knowledge set forth in the National Council of Teachers of Mathematics standards for middle-level students would be the minimum level of mathematics knowledge required of teachers for the elementary grades. High-school

---

[10]A "grade level category" is defined here as one of the three major divisions prevalent in K-12 education today: elementary, middle, and secondary.

[11]In the United States, many but not all elementary schools contain grades K-5, while many middle schools are for students in grades 6-8. It should be noted, however, that the *National Science Education Standards* (*NSES*) call for grouping of content knowledge and understanding for grades K-4, 5-8, and 9-12. Thus, in the middle band (grades 5-8), some of the science content called for in the *NSES* might be taught at different schools.

teachers of science and mathematics would have deep understanding of what is taught through first-year courses in their subject areas at colleges and universities. It should be noted that acquiring the desirable depth of understanding at any level usually will require advanced study of the pertinent subject matter. The content suggested for each major grade level category in the *National Science Education Standards* (NRC, 1996a) and by the *Principles and Standards for School Mathematics* (NCTM, 2000) are provided in Appendix B. A forthcoming publication from the Conference Board of the Mathematical Sciences (see footnote 9) also will address issues of teacher education for prospective teachers of mathematics.

However, despite the seemingly straightforward guidance reviewed above, the question of what content teachers need is deceptively multifaceted and complex. Level of content knowledge typically has been defined by the specific number of hours of science content or mathematics content coursework that must be a part of prospective teachers' preparation. At the elementary school level, this might be one to three courses, which, depending on the teacher education program or specific state requirements may or may not be tailored to prospective teachers at this grade level. At the secondary level, a teacher who teaches biology might be required to complete courses or demonstrate competency in genetics, ecology, physiology, microbiology, and conservation principles. That teacher also needs to acquire some breadth of knowledge in the other sciences, as well as in mathematics. Some states require a major or at least a minor in the appropriate field but may not articulate the details of specific subjects a teacher is expected to have studied nor the minimum hours of coursework required. To push more prospective teachers toward adequate content preparation, some states have limited the number of hours a candidate can take in education as part of the bachelor degree. For example, in 1999, the Colorado state legislature adopted the following conditions for teacher licensure, including at the elementary grades:

1. a teacher preparation option must be available to students to complete as undergraduates;
2. the bachelor's degree shall consist of no more than 120 semester hours; all candidates must complete an academic/ subject matter major and other general education requirements; and
3. the program shall include a minimum of 800 hours of organized and supervised school-based experiences.

Currently, in Texas, the teacher preparation component of a student's baccalaureate program (excluding student teaching) can account for no more than 18 semester hours. Other states, such as New York, have moved to a required five-year program, thereby ensuring that candidates have strong preparation in a major followed by a coherent teacher preparation program. In addition, a recent report from the American Federation of Teachers (2000) recommended that education for prospective teachers be organized as a five-year process at a minimum. Clearly, some policymakers believe that teachers' knowledge of content in a subject area is important to successful teaching and to successful student learning, although how this is put into practice and interpreted varies widely among the states.

It is important to keep in mind that when one examines the evidence of what it takes to teach science or mathematics well, increasing the teaching of content alone, without regard to how and in what context that content is taught, is insufficient. For example, the knowledge base in many fields of science, mathematics, and technology is growing and changing so rapidly that specific content that a student learns during preparation for teaching may be out-of-date or may need to be revised substantially by the time that person begins teaching. Teaching prospective teachers content knowledge without helping them also to understand how to keep abreast of developments in their subject area cannot lead to effective teaching of these disciplines.

Science and mathematics educators agree that strong content preparation is necessary but also look at the way that content is taught. The *National Science Education Standards* (NRC, 1996a) state

> Teachers of science will be the representatives of the science community in their classrooms, and they form much of their image of science through the science courses they take in college. If that image is to reflect the nature of science as presented in the standards, prospective and practicing teachers must take science courses in which they learn science through inquiry, having the same opportunities as their students will have to develop understanding.

The recently released content or "core" standards from the Interstate New Teacher Assessment and Support Consortium (INTASC, 1999) reinforce this recommendation by specifying that teachers of science and mathematics need to understand content as well as know how to apply that content in problem-solving and inquiry-based situations in the classroom. The principles from INTASC's *Core Standards* state further that all beginning teachers in science should have more laboratory experience than they can acquire through the lab-oriented courses currently offered to prospective teachers at many colleges and universities as shown in Table 3-1.

TABLE 3-1 INTASC Core Principle #1 on Expectations of Teachers' Content Knowledge

Principle Number 1:

The teacher understands the central concepts, tools of inquiry, and structures of the discipline(s) he or she teaches and can create learning experiences that make these aspects of subject matter meaningful for students.

Knowledge

The teacher understands major concepts, assumptions, debates, processes of inquiry, and ways of knowing that are central to the discipline(s) s/he teaches.

The teacher understands how students' conceptual frameworks and their misconceptions for an area of knowledge can influence their learning.

The teacher can relate his/her disciplinary knowledge to other subject areas.

Dispositions

The teacher realizes that subject matter knowledge is not a fixed body of facts but is complex and ever evolving. S/he seeks to keep abreast of new ideas and understandings in the field.

The teacher appreciates multiple perspectives and conveys to learners how knowledge is developed from the vantage point of the knower.

The teacher has enthusiasm for the discipline(s) s/he teaches and sees connections to everyday life.

The teacher is committed to continuous learning and engages in professional discourse about subject matter knowledge and children's learning of the discipline.

Performances

The teacher effectively uses multiple representations and explanations of disciplinary concepts that capture key ideas and link them to students' prior understandings.

The teacher can represent and use differing viewpoints, theories, "ways of knowing," and methods of inquiry in his/her teaching of subject matter concepts.

The teacher can evaluate teaching resources and curriculum materials for their comprehensiveness, accuracy, and usefulness for representing particular ideas and concepts.

The teacher engages students in generating knowledge and testing hypotheses according to the methods of inquiry and standards of evidence used in the discipline.

The teacher develops and uses curricula that encourage students to see, question, and interpret ideas from diverse perspectives.

The teacher can create interdisciplinary learning experiences that allow students to integrate knowledge, skills, and methods of inquiry from several subject areas.

Source: INTASC *Core Standards,* Council of Chief State School Officers.
Available at <http://www.ccsso.org/intascst.html>.

The recently released *Inquiry and the National Science Education Standards* (National Research Council, 2000a) puts it another way: "Programs are needed that explicitly attend to inquiry—both as a learning outcome for teachers and as a way for teachers to learn science subject matter."

But what research exists to support this recent emphasis upon knowing, understanding, and being able to do science and mathematics? Ball (1998) contended that, to teach mathematics effectively, a teacher must have knowledge of mathematics and a conceptual understanding of the principles underlying its topics, rules, and definitions. Ball (1990) and then Cooney (1994) also stated that content knowledge must be a central focus and an integral part of a mathematics teacher's preparation program. Similarly, after an extensive review of science education, Coble and Koballa (1996) concluded that science content must be the centerpiece of the preparation of science teachers. The major ideas of science "should form the core of the science content knowledge of all teachers, with depth of understanding reflected in the teacher's chosen level of teaching."

THE NATURE AND IMPORTANCE OF CONTENT KNOWLEDGE IN THE EDUCATION OF TEACHERS OF SCIENCE AND MATHEMATICS

What science or mathematics should a teacher know to be an effective teacher in these disciplines and subject areas? According to Shulman and Grossman (1988), content knowledge consists of an understanding of key facts, concepts, principles, and the frameworks of a discipline, as well as the rules of evidence and proof that are part of that discipline.

In an extensive review of the literature on the education of science teachers, Anderson and Mitchener (1994) noted that most preparation in subject matter occurs *outside* of schools of education. Prospective secondary science and mathematics teachers devote a large portion of their studies to their particular disciplines, but little is known about what students really learn in their subject area courses. This lack of knowledge about the real value of courses is particularly interesting in light of the fact that students in teacher education spend the majority of their academic time taking courses in the arts and sciences departments.

Ball (1990) and Borko et al. (1993) contended that teachers do not develop a deep understanding of mathematics during their own K-12 education or even in their undergraduate coursework. Even today, college coursework in mathematics may not stress conceptual understanding of content. Rather, the emphasis is on performing mathematical manipulations in a lecture format. Science coursework often is similar. Arons (1990) pointed out that college science courses, particularly introductory survey courses, focus on the major achievements in an area of science. Then, when prospective teachers of science go on in science coursework—most often some of the same coursework engaged in by science majors—they are exposed to science as a body of facts, not, as Coble and Koballa found more recently (1996), as a way of knowing the natural world through inquiry.[12]

Until recently, many teacher educators have taken it for granted that teacher candidates would be knowledgeable about subject matter in the discipline(s) in which they elected to major. Beyond reports that noted the number of courses taken at the college level by candidates, Cooney (1994) and Manouchehri (1997) could find no studies on the kinds or levels of secondary teachers' knowledge of mathemat-

ics. Moreover, research on the relationships between teachers' actual content knowledge (vs. amount of pedagogical training and experience) and the amount of student learning that occurs usually has been inconclusive.

Some recent studies do, however, point to a relationship between teachers' content background and the quality of their instruction. Reviews of the research on this subject (Fennema and Franke, 1992; Manouchehri, 1997) indicate that the importance of teachers' actual knowledge of content in mathematics and their conceptual understanding of mathematics in particular is coming under focused study. As early as 1985, Steinberg et al. found that teachers with deeper conceptual understanding also engaged students in active problem solving, and helped students see relationships inside and outside of mathematics. These authors suggested that there is a relationship between the quality of secondary teachers' knowledge of mathematics and the quality of their classroom instruction. More recent studies have confirmed the strong positive relationship between a teacher's conceptual understanding of mathematics and the choices he or she

---

[12]Undergraduate science, mathematics, and engineering education has begun to change during the past decade in ways that are consistent with the reforms being espoused for grades K-12. Rothman and Narum (1999) provide an overview of these changes in undergraduate education and predict the kinds of change that is likely over the next 10 years. Additional information about this report is available at <http://www.pkal.org/news/thennow100.html>.

makes in his or her instruction.

Brown and Borko (1992) concluded that teaching mathematics from a conceptual perspective is very unlikely to occur unless a teacher has deep conceptual understanding of the mathematics subject matter at hand. Later, Manouchehri (1997) stated flatly that the research literature supports the notion that "in the absence of conceptual understanding of content, effective teaching is highly improbable."

Few parallel studies exist for science education. Carlsen (1988) found that teachers with deeper conceptual understanding of science allowed their students to engage in discourse more often than teachers with weaker conceptual backgrounds. Carlsen also noted that teachers with greater understanding of content asked students a greater number of high-level questions, whereas teachers who did not know the material tended to dominate the classroom discussion.

Hashweh (1987) studied the effects of teachers' knowledge of subject matter in biology and physics on teachers' abilities to teach these subjects. He found that teachers with higher levels of content knowledge integrated pieces of that knowledge more often into their teaching. These teachers also recognized higher order principles in the discipline, and their instructional strategies reflected this depth of knowledge.

Within their specialty, teachers with greater content knowledge wrote examination questions that focused less on recall and more on students being able to apply and transfer information. However, when they were teaching outside of their specialty, these teachers followed textbook chapters more closely and were less likely to recognize or address student misconceptions. Hashweh concluded that knowledge of subject matter contributed greatly to these teachers' ability to translate a written curriculum into an active curriculum in biology and physics.

As was noted earlier in this report, some policymakers and teacher educators believe that prospective teachers should emphasize their preparation in subject matter at the expense of preparation in education. Do teachers who were majors in science or mathematics understand the subjects they teach better than teachers who were education majors? Ball and Wilson (1990) conducted a study at Michigan State University that examined this question with prospective elementary teachers before and after they had completed their teacher preparation programs. They looked at two groups, one composed of prospective teachers who had been prepared in a traditional preparation program, and the other composed of prospective teachers who had been prepared in an alternative program.

Their focus was the influence of these programs on the prospective teachers' teaching of mathematics. Ball and Wilson found that both groups of teacher candidates lacked understanding of the underlying relationships of mathematics. At the beginning of their teacher preparation programs, 60 percent of these prospective teachers could not generate a real-world example that would demonstrate to their students an application for the division of fractions. Moreover, they still could not generate an appropriate representation of division of fractions after they had graduated from their respective preparation programs. Ball and Wilson (1990) concluded that neither group was prepared to teach mathematics for understanding or to teach mathematics in ways that differ from "telling and drilling algorithms into students."

What else, then, needs to take place in teacher education programs to support candidates adequately in the effective teaching of science and/or mathematics? Several possible answers were revealed in a study of teachers' understanding of mathematics conducted recently by Ma (1999). Ma studied groups of elementary school teachers in China and the United States. Despite China's more limited teacher preparation program, Ma found that the Chinese teachers had a more profound understanding[13] of the mathematics they were teaching. This deeper understanding both of mathematics content and its application allowed Chinese teachers to promote mathematical learning and inquiry more effectively than their counterparts in the United States, especially when students raised novel ideas or claims that were outside the scope of the lesson being presented in class.

Ma's study provides some insights that might guide an upgrading of teacher knowledge in the United States. Specifically, most of the Chinese teachers only taught mathematics, up to three or four classes per day. Much of the rest of their day was unencumbered, allowing for reflection on their teaching and, perhaps more importantly, for shared study and conversation with fellow teachers about content and how to teach it. Their teaching assignments also permitted them to gain over time a better grasp of the entire elementary

---

[13]Ma (1999) described the following characteristics as evidence for a teacher's "profound understanding of mathematics": 1. The ability to sequence appropriately the introduction of new concepts; 2. The ability to make careful choices about problem types to be given to students in terms of number, context, and difficulty; 3. Brief but significant opportunities for students to encounter conceptual obstacles; 4. Solicitation from and discussion by students of multiple points of view about a problem; 5. Anticipation of more complex and related structures; 6. Powerful and timely introduction of generalizations.

school curriculum for mathematics. None of these features—specialist teachers in elementary schools, time for learning collaboratively with other teachers, and experience at a variety of grade levels—is common to U.S. elementary schools.

The kind and quality of teachers' inservice education can make a difference in how their students achieve. Cohen and Hill (1998) reported on a large-scale study of mathematics teachers in California who participated in a sustained program of professional development. Although this study actually focused on the effects of educational policy, it revealed important information about the opportunities that teachers need both to learn and to teach new state-required mathematics content as a means of enhancing student achievement. Using data from a 1994 survey of California elementary school teachers and student scores from the 1994 California Learning Assessment System (CLAS), this study examined whether students who are taught by teachers with more extensive opportunities for inservice education would perform better than students whose teachers had less extensive opportunities for inservice. "More extensive" was defined as *ongoing* opportunities to learn subject matter deeply, adopt new curriculum, and learn about appropriate and aligned assessments of student

learning and achievement. "Less extensive" was defined as participation in special topic workshops. Cohen and Hill (1998) found that the more time teachers spent in curriculum workshops, including those with opportunities to examine new curriculum with other teachers, the more reform-oriented and less conventional was their teaching practice. In fact, the difference was nearly 0.75 standard deviation higher, a statistically significant difference.

These results also appeared to be associated with student achievement. After taking student characteristics and school conditions into account, there was a modest positive correlation between the degree to which teachers reported that their classroom practice was oriented to California's state Mathematics Framework and average student scores on the CLAS. Cohen and Hill (1998) noted in particular the fact of the teachers' involvement with such work as writing topic units potentially to substitute for or elaborate on less in-depth textbook treatments. In addition, these teachers were involved in the construction of rubrics for assessing student responses to open-ended kinds of problems. No similar relationship was found for these two variables in schools where teachers engaged in a high degree of conventional practice.

Other studies have produced similar results. For example, another study of student achievement in California demonstrated that when teachers had experienced extended inservice opportunities to learn about mathematics curriculum and instruction, their students' achievement increased (Wiley and Yoon, 1995). Also, a study of mathematics reform, Quantitative Understanding: Amplifying Student Achievement and Reasoning (QUASAR), program found higher achievement among students whose teachers were involved in a sustained program of curriculum development, in this case, a program that emphasized enhancing teachers' understanding of strategies, having teachers implement new strategies, and encouraging teachers to reflect on instructional outcomes (Brown et al., 1995).[14]

In addition, Grouws and Schultz (1996) summarized a series of studies designed to gauge the impact of the University of Wisconsin's Cognitively Guided Instruction (CGI) research program for mathematics teacher effectiveness. According to Grouws and Schultz, the studies found that providing teachers with knowledge of how students think and opportunities to develop strategies in specific content domains changed teaching behaviors and improved student learning. In one study of first- and second-grade teachers, the CGI group provided teachers with knowledge of young children's thinking and with strategies for teaching addition and subtraction. Subsequently, these teachers spent more time in their mathematics instruction on problem solving and assessing student thinking than a control group of teachers who received equivalent hours of inservice training. The students of CGI teachers also performed better in some math assessments—higher in problem solving, comparably on computational tasks.

In their review, Grouws and Schultz specifically note a certain type of teacher knowledge, called pedagogical content knowledge (Shulman, 1986). They state, "In mathematics, pedagogical content knowledge includes, but is not limited to, useful representations, unifying ideas, clarifying examples and counterexamples, helpful analogies, important relationships, and connections among ideas. Thus, pedagogical content knowledge is a subset of content knowledge that has particular utility for planning and conducting lessons that facilitate student learning."

All of the studies cited in this chapter, as well as those cited earlier (e.g., Fetler, 1999), lend strong support to the idea that when teachers receive high-

---

[14]Information about the QUASAR program is available at <http://www.ed.gov/pubs/math/part6.html>.

quality preparation and engage in rich professional development, their understanding of education reform and the strategies underlying that reform is enhanced. However, it is clear that even the best teachers by themselves will be unable to make the kinds of inroads in improving student learning and academic achievement that are being expected across the United States. Their efforts must be supported by school and policy infrastructure, policies, and priorities that offer to teachers opportunities for continuing professional development and growth and that provide the facilities and resources necessary to encourage teaching and learning. Teachers also need good working conditions in order to thrive as professionals. The next chapter discusses the kinds of recommendations that professional organizations for teaching and in the various science and mathematics disciplines have issued for improving teacher education.

4
Recommendations from the Profession and the Disciplines

Over the past decade, an increasing number of research studies have been devoted to understanding and documenting how best to educate teachers of science and mathematics. Recommendations based on this research, based on proposals articulated by numerous organizations, and based on the realities of today's classrooms have been emerging since the early 1990s. Individual teaching professional associations, such as the National Science Teachers Association (1996, 1998), the National Council of Teachers of Mathematics (1991, 2000), the National Association of Biology Teachers (1990), and the Association for the Education of Teachers of Science (1997), have offered a variety of recommendations related to teaching science generally or in specific disciplines. Broader-based groups, such as the National Center for Improving Science Education (Raizen and Michelsohn, 1994), the American

Council on Education (1999), the National Research Council (1996a, 1999h), the National Science Foundation (1996), and the National Commission on Mathematics and Science Teaching for the 21st Century (2000) have issued their own recommendations for improving teacher education.

In addition, since 1994, the American Association for the Advancement of Science's Project 2061 has conducted hundreds of workshops across the nation with thousands of teachers, administrators, and university faculty. The programs emphasize cross-grade and cross-disciplinary participation, as well as the use of clear and explicit benchmarks for learning and the alignment of curriculum, instruction, and assessment to those benchmarks.

The *National Science Education Standards* (NRC, 1996a) provided a synthesis of recommendations designed specifically for science teacher education and professionalism (see also Appendix C and Appendix A, respectively). That effort followed extensive work on mathematics content and teaching standards by both the National Council of Teachers of Mathematics (NCTM, 1989, 1991) and the Mathematical Sciences Education Board of the NRC (1989, 1990), including recommendations for the preparation of mathematics teachers (see also Appendix C).

Taken together, the visions and recommendations of all the above-mentioned organizations paint a picture of teacher education as a complex, career-long process that involves the continual intellectual growth and professionalism of teachers, both individually and collectively. Acknowledged is that teacher education can and does occur in a variety of ways and involves many different kinds of people, both inside and outside of college, and in school classrooms. Emphasized is the need for approaches to teacher education that employ methods of inquiry, classroom discourse, and other standards—recommended teaching strategies that both reflect and guide what teachers will be expected to use in the classroom with their own students. Understood is that learning to teach science, mathematics, and technology effectively very much depends on teachers mastering the content of these disciplines and having opportunities to practice their pedagogical content knowledge within school environments.

One of my previous ideas about inquiry was that it consisted mainly of doing laboratory activities. I discovered that, although labs can aid in the process of sense-making, they often don't because they are either "cookbook" (they don't allow the students to make choices or judgments) or "confirmatory" (they follow lectures or students' reading). What I have realized is that the essence of inquiry does not lie in any elaborate, equipment-intensive laboratory exercise. It lies, rather, in the interactions between the student and the materials, as well as in the teacher-student and student-student interactions that occur dozens of times each and every class period.

Vignette of reflection from a high school physics teacher
National Research Council, 2000b, page 90

During the past decade, two nationally based organizations have been studying the competencies that should characterize accomplished teachers and teachers who have recently entered the profession. The National Board of Professional Teaching Standards (NBPTS), formed in the late 1980s, established five guiding principles for assessing the competence of experienced teachers (see Table 4-1). With these principles in place, the Council of Chief State School Officers then established the Interstate New Teacher Assessment and Support Consortium (INTASC), which developed a parallel set of core standards for novice teachers, as discussed earlier (see Table 3-1). Currently, more than 30 states are members of INTASC, an organization compelled by the premise that "the complex art of teaching requires performance-based standards and assessment strategies that are capable of capturing teachers' reasoned judgments and that evaluate what they can actually do in authentic teaching situations" (INTASC, 1999).

By establishing expectations for both accomplished and novice teachers, respectively, the recommendations from NBPTS and INTASC offer visions and guidance about how teachers of science and mathematics could be educated. A synthesis of the NBPTS and INTASC recommendations, as well as those of disciplinary societies and related organizations, suggest that teacher education programs in science and mathematics should exhibit the following characteristics:

• Be collaborative endeavors developed and conducted by scientists, mathematicians, education faculty, and practicing K-12 teachers with assistance from members of professional organizations and science- and mathematics-rich businesses and industries;

• Help prospective teachers to know well, understand deeply, and use effectively and creatively the fundamental content and concepts of the disciplines that they will teach. This includes understanding the disciplines from personal and social perspectives. It also includes being familiar with the disciplines' history and nature, unifying concepts, and the processes of inquiry and design that practitioners of the disciplines use in discovering and applying new knowledge;

• Unify, coordinate, and connect content courses in science, mathematics, or technology with methods courses and field experiences. They also should enhance teachers' proficiency in teaching over time through continuous experiences that help them address varying student interests and backgrounds;

• Teach content through the perspectives and methods of inquiry and prob-

TABLE 4-1 The "Five Principles of Accomplished Teaching" as Proposed by the National Board for Professional Teaching Standards

1. Teachers are committed to students and their learning.

Accomplished teachers are dedicated to making knowledge accessible to all students. They act on the belief that all students can learn. They treat students equitably, recognizing the individual differences that distinguish one student from another and taking account of these differences in their practice. They adjust their practice based on observation and knowledge of their students' interests, abilities, skills, knowledge, and family circumstances and peer relationships.

Accomplished teachers understand how students develop and learn. They incorporate the prevailing theories of cognition and intelligence in their practice. They are aware of the influence of context and culture on behavior. They develop students' cognitive capacity and their respect for learning. Equally important, they foster students' self-esteem, motivation, character, civic responsibility and their respect for individual, cultural, religious and racial differences.

2. Teachers know the subjects they teach and how to teach those subjects to students.

Accomplished teachers have a rich understanding of the subject(s) they teach and appreciate how knowledge in their subject is created, organized, linked to other disciplines and applied to real-world settings. While faithfully representing the collective wisdom of our culture and upholding the value of disciplinary knowledge, they also develop the critical and analytical capacities of their students.

Accomplished teachers command specialized knowledge of how to convey and reveal subject matter to students. They are aware of the preconceptions and background knowledge that students typically bring to each subject and of strategies and instructional materials that can be of assistance. They understand where difficulties are likely to arise and modify their practice accordingly. Their instructional repertoire allows them to create multiple paths to the subjects they teach, and they are adept at teaching students how to pose and solve their own problems.

3. Teachers are responsible for managing and monitoring student learning.

Accomplished teachers create, enrich, maintain and alter instructional settings to capture and sustain the interest of their students and to make the most effective use of time. They also are adept at engaging students and adults to assist their teaching and at enlisting their colleagues' knowledge and expertise to complement their own.

Accomplished teachers command a range of generic instructional techniques, know when each is appropriate and can implement them as needed. They are as aware of ineffectual or damaging practice as they are devoted to elegant practice.

They know how to engage groups of students to ensure a disciplined learning environment, and how to organize instruction to allow the schools' goals for students to be met. They are adept at setting norms for social interaction among students and between students and teachers. They understand how to motivate students to learn and how to maintain their interest even in the face of temporary failure. Accomplished

continued

teachers can assess the progress of individual students as well as that of the class as a whole. They employ multiple methods for measuring student growth and understanding and can clearly explain student performance to parents.

4. Teachers think systematically about their practice and learn from experience.

Accomplished teachers are models of educated persons, exemplifying the virtues they seek to inspire in students—curiosity, tolerance, honesty, fairness, respect for diversity and appreciation of cultural differences—and the capacities that are prerequisites for intellectual growth: the ability to reason and take multiple perspectives, to be creative and take risks, and to adopt an experimental and problem-solving orientation.

Accomplished teachers draw on their knowledge of human development, subject matter and instruction, and their understanding of their students to make principled judgments about sound practice. Their decisions are not only grounded in the literature, but also in their experience. They engage in lifelong learning, which they seek to encourage in their students.

Striving to strengthen their teaching, accomplished teachers critically examine their practice, seek to expand their repertoire, deepen their knowledge, sharpen their judgment and adapt their teaching to new findings, ideas and theories.

5. Teachers are members of learning communities.

Accomplished teachers contribute to the effectiveness of the school by working collaboratively with other professionals on instructional policy, curriculum development and staff development. They can evaluate school progress and the allocation of school resources in light of their understanding of state and local educational objectives. They are knowledgeable about specialized school and community resources that can be engaged for their students' benefit, and are skilled at employing such resources as needed.

Accomplished teachers find ways to work collaboratively and creatively with parents, engaging them productively in the work of the school.

Source: Council of Chief State School Officers. See <http://www.nbpts.org/nbpts/standards/intro.html>

lem solving, as well as illustrate and model in content courses, methods courses, and school-based field experiences a wide variety of effective teaching and assessment strategies that are consistent with the national education standards for science, mathematics, and technology;

- Present content in ways that allow students to appreciate the applications of science, mathematics, and technology, such as collecting, processing, and communicating information and statistical analysis and interpretation of data;
- Provide learning experiences in which science, mathematics, and tech-

nology are related to and integrated with students' interests, community concerns, and societal issues, as well as provide opportunities for collaborative learning experiences where students work in teams or groups and also to have significant and substantial involvement in scientific research;

• Integrate education theory with actual teaching practice, and knowledge from science and mathematics teaching experience with research on how people learn science and mathematics;

• Provide opportunities for prospective teachers to learn about and practice teaching in a variety of school contexts and with diverse groups of children, as well as provide opportunities for these teachers to practice and apply what they are learning in supportive environments that offer continual feedback, modeling of quality teaching practices, and individual coaching from faculty, practitioners, mentors, and peers;

• Encourage reflective inquiry into teaching through individual and collaborative study, discussion, assessment, experimentation, analysis, classroom-based research, and practice; and

• Welcome students into the professional community of educators and promote a professional vision of teaching by providing opportunities for experienced and future teachers to assume new roles and leadership positions, generate and apply new knowledge, and facilitate improvement efforts.

Given this wealth of reports and recommendations during the past decade, have institutions of higher education, individual schools, and school districts heeded these recommendations and actually instituted changes in their programs for teacher preparation and professional development? Is teacher education better now as a result of these calls for reform? These questions are addressed more fully in the next chapter.

5
Teacher Education as a Professional Continuum

Given the critical need for well-qualified teachers of science and mathematics, it is sobering to consider current statistics regarding the teaching profession in the United States. Nearly 50 percent of all students who currently enter preservice programs in college and universities do not pursue teaching as a career. Of those who do become certified as teachers and then enter the profession, nearly 30 percent leave within the first five years of practice (Darling-Hammond and Berry, 1998; Henderson, 2000). The problems are exacerbated for prospective and beginning teachers of science and mathematics (U.S. Department of Education, 1997a).

What are some of the implications of these statistics? To varying degrees, some states across the country are experiencing a reduction in the number of "in field" or experienced teachers

available for or hired to work in their larger school districts. In California alone, legislatively mandated reductions in class sizes, expectations that all students will study more science and mathematics, the high attrition rate of science and mathematics teachers, and the inability to hire sufficient numbers of certified teachers in these disciplines has resulted in a dire situation: approximately one-third of children in that state are being taught by teachers who either are unqualified to teach science or mathematics or are in their first or second year of teaching. Indeed, in California, the probability that a student who attends school in a low socioeconomic district will be taught by a less-than-qualified teacher can be five times higher than for students in more affluent districts in that state (Shields et al., 1999[1]). Across the country there also is

---

[1]This report also is available on-line at <http://www.cftl.org>.

... in addition to teacher preparation, we have the continuing challenge of professional development, where school districts update the knowledge, skills, and strategies that teachers bring into the classroom. No professional is equipped to practice for all time, i.e., be an inexhaustible "vein of gold." We cannot expect world-class student learning of mathematics and science if U.S. teachers lack the confidence, enthusiasm, and knowledge to deliver world-class instruction.

National Science Board, 1999, page 7

a higher probability that students in districts with large populations of underrepresented minorities or with high levels of poverty will be taught by unqualified or inexperienced teachers. Yet, in some states and districts, there are more qualified applicants for teaching positions in science and mathematics than there are jobs. As a result of these statistics and demographic research, some have claimed that, at least for now, the issue of teacher shortages is actually a problem of inequities in distribution, recruitment, and incentives (e.g., Darling-Hammond and Berry, 1998). Clearly, a method for addressing and ameliorating these various challenges, such as a coordinated and integrated system for locating and placing qualified teachers in school districts across the country, is lacking at the national level.

Why does this disjointed—and very worrisome—situation exist? The earlier part of this report documented some of the challenges that prospective teachers face. Those who then enter and decide to remain in the profession face opportunities for professional development that are far from comprehensive or integrated. Indeed, they often must endure professional development "opportunities" that are disjointed, repetitive from year to year, unconnected to their practice in the classroom, and ephemeral. Professional development days sponsored by districts are typically one-time workshops conducted by outside facilitators who may know little about those teachers' educational needs or the problems they face in teaching (e.g., Loucks-Horsley and Matsumoto, 1999). Some states have stopped providing funds for professional development while others are demanding that teachers engage in even more professional development. In the latter case, states may or may not provide financial assistance for local districts to carry out their mandates.

SYSTEMIC APPROACHES TO IMPROVING TEACHER EDUCATION

Institutions of Higher Education: One Key

In *Tomorrow's Schools of Education*, the Holmes Group (1995) charged that "education students for too long have been learning too little of the right things in the wrong places at the wrong time." Their report challenged colleges of education to raise their standards and to make important changes in their curriculum, faculty, location of their work, and in their student body. Similarly, the Holmes Group exhorted, "The Universities that develop education knowledge, influence education policy, and prepare teachers and other leaders for our nation's schools and education schools must overcome 'business as usual' to meet the challenge of these truly unusual times in education. The indisputable link between the quality of elementary and secondary schools and the quality of the education schools must be acknowledged—and we must respond."

Other high-level reports have echoed the conclusions of this and the other Holmes Group reports (1986, 1990). In 1996, an advisory committee to the National Science Foundation recommended that to improve the preparation of teachers and principals, schools of education should (1) build bridges to other departments, (2) look for ways to reinforce and integrate learning, rather than maintaining artificial barriers between courses in content and pedagogy, and (3) develop partnerships and collaborations with colleagues in education, in the K-12 sector, and in the business world (NSF, 1996). In 1999, the American Council on Education

---

While school reform alone cannot eliminate all the causes of educational failure in our society, a more responsive educational system is a vital step in breaking the cycle of failure that entraps too many of our students and teachers. Schools and universities must be willing to reexamine everything: the way they utilize personnel, space, money, time, research, and technology. They must creatively build different kinds of schools and preparation programs that bridge the gap between what is learned and what people need to understand and be able to do in order to be productive in the future.

Richardson, 1994, page 1

---

urged the presidents and chancellors of the nation's colleges and universities with education programs either to elevate the status of these programs so that the entire institution is concerned about their quality or eliminate them.

SOME EXEMPLARY APPROACHES TO TEACHER EDUCATION

Even as new recommendations for the education of teachers were emerging in the 1990s, teacher educators in this country already were exploring ways to improve their programs. The need for career-long professional development, combined with the need to restructure schools and teacher preparation programs, created a unique opportunity for collaborative approaches to systemic reform, where the many components of reform are addressed and their interdependencies and interrelationships are recognized (Goodlad, 1990, 1994; Holmes Group 1986, 1990, 1995). Many individual school districts and states have now recognized the critical connection between ongoing professional development during the induction and post-induction years of teaching. They also have begun to institute a variety of programs that professionally nurture and sustain beginning teachers during the first years of their careers beyond the induction period.

Descriptions of several of these programs are provided in Appendix D.

As noted throughout this report, there have been numerous calls for institutions of higher education to improve teacher education through enhanced communication among science and mathematics educators, scientists, and mathematicians. These calls for reform also have urged the creation of formal connections between institutions of higher education and public schools (e.g., Holmes Group, 1986; Goodlad, 1994). In keeping with this more systemic approach, a movement has been emerging slowly since the 1980s that seeks to improve simultaneously the education of both prospective and practicing teachers through partnerships between schools and postsecondary institutions.

Various labels have been applied to this movement and to the products that have emerged. These labels include "professional development schools," "clinical schools," "professional practice schools," "school-university partnerships," and "partnership schools" (Whitford and Metcalf-Turner, 1999). Professional Development School (PDS), the descriptor selected by the Holmes Group (1986), still predominates in the educational literature. It is the term this report will use to denote any intentional collaboration between a college or university and one or more

K-12 schools for teacher preparation and school renewal.

Such collaborative arrangements adhere to several important principles:

- They offer learning programs for diverse populations of students;
- They ground preparation for novice teachers in classroom practice;
- They articulate and establish consensus about professional goals and responsibilities for experienced educators; and
- Many conduct research that adds to educators' knowledge about how to make schools more effective and productive (Holmes Group, 1990).

These collaborative movements were established on the premise that a student's education should be viewed as an integrated continuum from preschool through university. When viewed in this light, significant improvement in any one part of the educational system in isolation can be seen as unlikely to have much effect on improving education in general unless concomitant improvements are made throughout the system. Thus, improvement in K-12 schools cannot be expected until the preparation of teachers and administrators improves at the university level. In turn, even the best teachers and administrators cannot be sustained professionally until the system becomes more effective in providing high-quality professional development and empowering those who have primary responsibility for educating children. Simultaneous and coordinated feedback and renewal are essential components of this movement (Goodlad, 1994).

An effective PDS, therefore, is much more than a collection of people in a building. "It entails an attitude, a perspective, a professional predisposition that releases educators to share what they know and to improve the teaching of students and the preparation of future educators" (Richardson, 1994). Participation in a PDS collaboration involves willingness by all of the partners to question old habits and new trends in education and to suggest different ways of reaching current and future goals. Professional Development Schools have become laboratories for observation, experimentation, and extended practice. A PDS can be a site where teachers, students, and university faculty create new knowledge and experiment with, evaluate, and revise practices. Ultimately, the PDS concept embodies a commitment to do what is necessary to ensure that all students (K-16) become engaged learners.

Like student learning, teacher education also is an extremely complex process. PDS collaborations encourage educators to restructure teacher education systemically rather than through a series of disjointed, incremental reforms. For example, a PDS offers to preservice and novice teachers systematic field experiences within realistically complex learning environments. By integrating content and pedagogy in an atmosphere of relevance for their studies, these experiences become a unifying feature of education for student teachers.

Currently, there are over 600 reported examples of partnerships between universities and school districts involving the PDS approach to educational reform (Abdal-Haqq, 1998).[2] Many more such programs may exist that are unreported or that employ some, but not all, of the principles of the PDS movement.

THE EFFECTIVENESS OF PDS AND SIMILAR COLLABORATIVE EFFORTS IN IMPROVING STUDENT LEARNING

Although the PDS movement is still relatively young, the research literature on Professional Development Schools is beginning to document the impact of high quality, focused professional development experiences for teachers on schools and students. Some encouraging examples of cases where this

connection does seem to be in effect have now been reported (e.g., reviews by Abdal-Haqq, 1998; Byrd and McIntyre, 1999). For example, in 1996, Trachtman conducted a survey of 28 "highly developed" PDS sites for the Professional Development Schools Standards Project.[3] Sixty-five percent of the responding sites indicated that preservice teachers affiliated with the sites in the PDS context spent more time in field-related experiences than teachers who were enrolled in more traditional teacher education programs. In PDS arrangements, preservice teachers usually are assigned to a teaching site in cohorts, a desirable practice according to other research. These cohorts work with school-based teams of teachers. Teacher teams have a variety of functions, including curriculum development, action research, creating performance assessments, and university teaching. These preservice teachers also assume building-wide responsibilities and other roles beyond their own classroom settings, thereby providing time for practicing teachers in the school to engage in other kinds of professional work.

According to a previous study by Houston et al. (1999), at more than 80

---

[2]In a presentation to the CSMTP in 1999, Abdal-Haqq reported that the number of PDS schools has risen to more than 1,000.

[3]Additional information about this project is available at <http://www.ncate.org/accred/projects/pds/m-pds.htm>.

percent of these sites teachers worked together with college faculty to plan curricula for improving teacher education at their collaborating institution of higher education as well as on site at their schools. More than 90 percent of the respondents reported that at least one preservice course was being taught directly at their school site. Further, at more than 50 percent of the sites, teachers from grades K-12 held adjunct or other similar kinds of college faculty appointments. At 60 percent of the sites, PDS classroom teachers participated in activities connected with the upgrading of university-level teacher education program renewal. Seventy-five percent of the sites surveyed indicated that the preservice teachers working with them also engaged in research about teaching practice. Finally, 89 percent of the respondents indicated that university and school faculty worked together to plan professional development activities (Houston et al., 1999).

According to anecdotal reports, graduates of PDS programs begin their professional careers with greater knowledge and more teaching skills than graduates of more traditional preservice programs. In addition, it has been observed that teachers trained in PDS environments have a greater understanding of the diversity and the nonacademic needs of students, are more committed to and self-confident about teaching, and are more likely to reach out to others and participate in school-wide activities (Houston et al., 1999).

Houston et al. (1999) also reported that in Texas, teacher candidates with PDS experience outperformed their peers by 15 to 34 percentage points in the state's required examination for teacher licensure, although the study authors acknowledged that it is unclear whether the difference in performance was due to PDS experience *per se* or to the qualities of students attracted to PDS programs.

There also is isolated statistical and anecdotal evidence that a higher percentage of PDS graduates remain in teaching. For example, in a study of the Model Clinical Teaching Program (MCTP), a PDS partnership between East Carolina University faculty and cooperating teachers in the Pitt County, NC schools was formed that included a full year of internship along with extensive and ongoing staff development. Of 60 MCTP graduates whose careers were followed after having completed this program, 96 percent continued as classroom teachers five, and in some cases, six years after entering the profession compared with a national average of less than 60 percent. After seven years of piloting this program, East Carolina University has now adopted it for the senior year of all of its teacher preparation programs (Parmalee Hawk, personal communication). In addition, these kinds of programs also influence student performance on standardized tests. On the North Carolina state-mandated test of comprehension skills, "PDS schools performed better than most other schools in the district and were above average for the state as a whole. Minimal skill scores for the middle-school students were higher than they had ever been, and mathematics scores for third and fifth graders also improved (Apple, 1997).

In Maryland, state law requires all teacher education candidates to spend a full-year interning in a PDS. The University of Maryland (UMD) is actively engaged in Professional Development Schools in the state, and while a study has yet to be conducted regarding efficacy, anecdotally, school superintendents and participating teachers have indicated that the program makes a positive difference (Martin Johnson, 2000, personal correspondence). In UMD Professional Development Schools, clusters of schools act as the K-12 partners; i.e., five or six elementary or five or six secondary and middle schools "held together by the concept of reform and renewal."

EDUCATING ELEMENTARY SCHOOL TEACHERS IN THE TEACHING OF SCIENCE AND MATHEMATICS: SPECIAL CONSIDERATIONS

Traditionally, most districts and states have expected teachers in the elementary grades to be generalists. Despite the accumulating evidence cited throughout this report that teachers need a deep knowledge and understanding of science and mathematics to teach these subjects effectively at any grade, education programs for people who teach in the primary grades typically emphasize and reinforce the notion of elementary teachers as non-specialists. Even in states that now require prospective elementary school teachers to major in a discipline other than education, few opt for majors in science or mathematics. Many reports have suggested, however, that teachers of *all* grade levels must understand deeply the subject matter that they teach and use this knowledge to teach what is appropriate to students at different grade levels (pedagogical content knowledge) if they are to be effective in the classroom (Shulman, 1987).

The idea that subject area specialists might be needed in elementary schools is not new. Following the publication of *A Nation at Risk* (National Commission on Excellence in Education, 1983), subsequent conversations among education specialists and members of professional disciplinary societies led to the development of additional recommendations. For example, participants at a 1993 conference sponsored by the U.S. Department of Education, the NCTM, and the Wisconsin Center for Education Research recommended that, in elementary schools, specialist teachers of mathematics teach all mathematics beginning no later than grade 4 and supervise mathematics instruction at earlier grade levels (Romberg, 1994).

In recent years, many elementary schools and their districts have begun to address the disconnect between how elementary school teachers have been prepared to teach science and mathematics and the critical need for teachers who have the knowledge and acumen to work effectively with younger children in these subject areas. A number of strategies have emerged. They include

1. recruiting teachers who have majored in science or mathematics to teach these subjects at the elementary level (similar to their counterparts in the secondary grades and, increasingly, in the middle grades). Because many science or mathematics majors have decided to enter teaching late in their undergraduate years or thereafter, many of these students may opt to teach in private schools where certification is not required;

2. training current employees or hiring teachers who can serve as content specialists in these subject areas. Depending on the size of the school or district, these content specialists may be responsible for teaching most of the science program in a school and may even travel among schools to do so (similar to teachers of art or music);

3. establishing "teaching pods" consisting of several teachers and the students they teach within a school. In this system, every teacher oversees one class of students. One teacher in the pod may take primary responsibility for teaching science or mathematics while other teachers focus on other subject areas. Depending on the school, teachers may rotate among the classes in the pod over the course of a day or several days. Conversely, if one classroom has been specially constructed for science, teachers may remain in a given classroom throughout the day while students rotate among the classrooms.

The issue of preparing content and pedagogical specialists in science and mathematics for teaching in the elementary grades persists, however. While elementary schools are being held increasingly responsible for improving teaching and learning in these disciplines, many current and prospective elementary school teachers continue to dislike and eschew teaching them. Given the current situation, it is difficult not to conclude that improvement in teacher preparation programs would help. For example, in a seminal report, the National Center for Improving Science Education (Raizen and Michelsohn, 1994) reported that one characteristic of effective elementary preservice teacher preparation is close professional collaboration among science faculty, education faculty, and experienced elementary school teachers. Raizen and Michelson went on to recommend at least informal collaboration between individuals and institutions on issues such as distribution requirements for students in teacher education programs.

On the basis of that report and subsequent recommendations from many other organizations, (e.g., NRC, 1996a, 1999h; NSF, 1996; ACE, 1999), it seems clear that joint planning of courses in pedagogy or science course content by science, mathematics, and engineering faculty, education faculty in these disciplines, and local classroom teachers should occur regularly. Even more desirable would be programs that integrate science content courses, methods courses, and field experiences.

Such programs also could include some form of collaborative research in which university faculty and classroom teachers investigate a problem focused on improving student learning or increasing the impact of a new curriculum.

Raizen and Michelsohn (1994) mentioned Professional Development Schools as the type of setting where such collaborative program planning, implementation, and research could take place. In PDS settings, experienced elementary school teachers can be both active and coequal partners with university faculty and work with student teachers. In this kind of environment, elementary school teachers can contribute greatly to a more well-rounded teacher education program.

The kinds of data discussed in this chapter and throughout this report make clear that teacher education, recruitment, and professional development in the United States must develop new ways of doing business. The education and policy communities need to reach consensus about systems for teacher education and recruitment that, like the medical school model, can be adopted nationally and adapted by states and localities to guide and support new teachers through their first crucial years on the job. The various stakeholders in teacher education also must find better ways to provide experienced teachers with meaningful, intellectually engaging opportunities for continual professional growth. At the same time, officials in schools and districts must recognize the emerging consensus that well-prepared teachers are critical for raising student achievement and should avoid the temptation to hire and staff their classrooms with unqualified or out-of-field teachers when personnel shortages loom.[4] Further, in light of the research findings presented throughout this report, school administrators and policymakers should find ways to utilize teachers in those subject areas where they exhibit strength, interest, and training. Teachers should not be asked to teach subjects outside of their areas of competence and interest even though their certification may allow them to do so. If teachers are asked to move to teaching in those other subject areas, then additional professional development should be a prerequisite for doing so.

The National Commission on Teaching and America's Future has concluded that just as businesses and industries invest in the development of their employees, so must schools, schools systems, and policymakers invest in the ongoing education and professional development of teachers. Educators from preschool through university,

parents, citizens, and students all must come to see themselves as essential stakeholders in the decisions and policies that affect the quality of education in America (Fuhrman and Massell, 1992).

Data from research and successful practice are demonstrating that it is critically important for certain groups of individuals and organizations to become actively engaged in the process of teacher education. At a minimum, these groups include faculty in mathematics, and the life, physical, and earth sciences in both two-year and four-year colleges, as well as teachers and administrators in K-12 schools. Collaborative partnerships appear to be particularly effective ways to realize improved teacher education, particularly when they involve scientists, mathematicians, and faculty from schools of education from two- and four-year colleges and universities and teachers from participating school systems (AAAS, 1989; MAA, 1991; NCTM, 1989; NRC, 1989, 1990, and 1996a; NSTA, 1998).

The data cited in this chapter point to some common themes about successful collaborative partnerships for the preparation and professional development of teachers and the enhancement

---

[4]A number of recent reports suggest that teacher shortages may be due in part (at least in the short-term) to inequitable distribution of the teacher workforce. Qualified teachers can be located and hired if they are offered the appropriate incentives and suitable working conditions (e.g., Darling-Hammond, 1998, and personal communication with the committee).

of learning by students. First, the professional community's level of effort, commitment, and input in a school can have significant effects on student achievement. Support from the larger community in which a school is located also can make a critical difference in the success of teachers and their students. This larger community includes the policymakers, superintendents, district administrators, teacher unions, faculty and administrators from local colleges and universities, individual school staff, and other members of the community, such as leaders of local businesses and industry. It also includes scientists and mathematicians outside of academe, who can bring their understanding and everyday applications of science and mathematics concepts and skills to K-12 teaching and learning improvement. When these institutions work together as a whole, make decisions that are supportive and collegial, and invest the time and money that it takes to make a concrete impact on education, teachers are afforded the opportunity to greatly enhance their teaching practice.

Second, this enhancement in teaching practice, in turn, appears to influence positively the scholastic achievement of students and their attitudes towards learning. In schools where teachers reported higher levels of collective responsibility for student learning, learning was greater in science, math-

ematics, reading, and history (Newmann and Wehlage, 1995).

Third, the comprehensive approach to teacher education appears to be promising. Professional Development Schools and similar collaborative programs attempt to address teacher preparation, professional development, and student learning holistically. They encourage teacher educators and prospective teachers to see themselves as students of learning as well as students of teaching. Research suggests that teachers who develop this level of professionalism are better able to respond to the constant and fluctuating demands of their jobs. McCullough and Mintz (1992), Lampert and Ball (1998), and McIntyre et al. (1996) all have pointed to the need for preservice preparation that encourages reflective practice. For example, McIntyre et al. (1996) concluded, "Student teachers within this framework view teaching as ongoing decision-making rather than as a product or recipe. These student teachers learn that significant education must present learners with relevant problematic situations in which the learner can manipulate objects to see what happens, to question what is already known, to compare their findings and assumptions with those of others, and to search for their own answers."

In summary, the committee has concluded that the collaborative and holistic perspective on teacher education and student learning represented by Professional Development Schools epitomizes what is required for comprehensive teacher education. The attributes exhibited by PDS programs and other similar collaborative efforts should be viewed as integral components of *all* teacher education programs.

This is not enough, however. Based on its two years of study, the committee also has concluded that improvement of teacher education for science, mathematics, and technology will require greater levels of cooperation among the various stakeholders than is currently the case even among Professional Development Schools. Sustainable change will require some fundamental rethinking of the roles and strengths of each of the organizations involved in the partnerships, including the allocation or reallocation of human and financial resources from each of the partners. In the next chapter of this report, the committee presents its broad vision for improving teacher education, including concepts for how those who are involved in teacher education might rethink and redefine their roles. Recommendations for implementing this vision conclude the main report.

6
A Vision for Improving Teacher Education and the Teaching Profession

As noted throughout this report, numerous commissions, committees, and state and national organizations have recently addressed the need for improving the teaching of science and mathematics in the United States and, hence, the preparation and professional development of teachers in these disciplines. The Committee on Science and Mathematics Teacher Preparation (CSMTP) has reached similar conclusions. Committee members strongly support the idea that leaders in national, state, and local governments, and all education communities must declare that the improvement of teacher education is a top priority. Most critically, our nation's colleges and universities must embrace this imperative. Committee members concur with the recent statements of the American Council on Education (1999), the Presidents and Chancellors of the Association of American Universities (1999), and U.S. Secretary of Education Richard Riley (1998, 2000) regarding the role of higher education in improving teacher education: *teacher education must become a central focus of the entire institution, not just of schools or departments of education.* The committee also strongly supports the specific recommendation from the American Council on Education (1999), *"Where teacher education programs operate at the periphery of the institution's strategic interests and directions, they should be moved to the center—or moved out."*

The CSMTP's examination of research data, recommendations, and current practices also has convinced members that significant improvement in recruiting, preparing, inducting, and retaining teachers for the teaching of science and mathematics in grades K-12 demands fundamental changes in our current systems of teacher education. Small adjustments cannot and will not

Improving teacher quality is at the heart of our national effort to achieve excellence in the classroom. This comes at a time when the very structure of education is going through a profound change. With knowledge all around us, available anytime and anywhere, the role of the teacher is going to be fundamentally transformed in the 21st century.

In the future, schools will be more fluid, teachers more adaptable and flexible, and students will be more accountable as the task of learning becomes theirs. The challenge of the modern classroom is its increasing diversity and the skills that this diversity requires of teachers. This is why we need to do some new thinking when it comes to the teaching profession.

We need a dramatic overhaul of how we recruit, prepare, induct and retain good teachers. The status quo is not good enough. And we must revamp professional development as we know it. New distance learning models can be powerful new tools to give teachers more opportunities to be better teachers.

Our efforts to improve education will rise or fall on the quality of our teaching force, and higher education has the defining role in preparing the next generation of teachers. I ask leaders in higher education across the nation to please make this their mission.

Richard Riley, U.S. Secretary of Education, 2000

Not long ago, a college chemistry professor grew angry with the way her daughter's high school chemistry class was being taught. She made an appointment to meet with the teacher and marched with righteous indignation into the classroom—only to discover that the teacher was one of her own former students.

Yates, 1995

result in sustainable improvement of science and mathematics. Nor will small changes improve science and mathematics teaching as a profession that attracts and retains the most qualified practitioners.

TEACHER EDUCATION IN THE 21ST CENTURY

Based on its findings and conclusions, CSMTP proposes a new level of partnership between K-12 schools and the higher education community that is designed to ensure high-quality teacher education. This teacher education model would stress and foster greater integration of the initial preparation of teachers and the professional education of teachers throughout their careers. Each college or university with a program designed to prepare college students for teacher certification and the teaching profession would enter into long-term partnerships with one or more school districts. The goal of these partnerships would be sharing the responsibilities of educating future teachers and providing ongoing professional development opportunities for the teachers in the participating K-12 schools.

In these new partnerships, master/mentor teachers in partner school districts would have adjunct appointments with the schools of education or the departments of science, mathematics, or engineering within the partner colleges or universities. These teachers would take on a significant role in the mentoring of future teachers during their practicum experiences. In turn, colleges and universities would assume a greater responsibility for providing professional development opportunities for teachers who teach in the partner school districts.

This arrangement would be a partnership in the truest sense, as college faculty and K-12 teachers would work together on a continuous basis to improve the teacher education process and to determine the on-going professional development needs of the teacher workforce in the partner school districts. At the collegiate level, the partnership would include active involvement by both education faculty and faculty from departments of science, mathematics, and engineering. Similarly, wherever it is the case that future teachers obtain a significant part of their education at community colleges, the partnership should involve both two- and four-year colleges.

The remainder of this chapter elaborates the committee's vision for these new partnerships.

ARTICULATION OF THE VISION

As a result of nearly two years of study and deliberation, the CSMTP proposes the following six *Guiding Principles*, which together constitute a new vision for improving teacher education in science, mathematics, and technology:

1. The improvement of teacher education and teaching in science, mathematics, and technology should be viewed as a top national priority.

2. Teacher education in science, mathematics, and technology must become a career-long process. High-quality professional development programs that include intellectual growth as well as the upgrading of teachers' knowledge and skills must be expected and essential features in the careers of all teachers.

3. Through changes in the rewards for, incentives for, and expectations of teachers, teaching as a profession must be upgraded in status and stature to the level of other professions.

4. Both individually and collectively, two- and four-year colleges and universities must assume greater responsibility and be held more accountable for improving teacher education.

5. Neither the higher education nor the K-12 communities can successfully improve teacher education as effectively in isolation as they can by working closely together. Collective, fully integrated efforts among school staff and administrators in individual schools and districts, teacher unions, faculty and administrators in institutions of higher education, policymakers from local colleges and universities, and parents are essential for addressing these issues.

6. Many more scientists, mathematicians, and engineers must become well informed enough to be involved with local and national efforts to provide the appropriate content knowledge and pedagogy of their disciplines to current and future teachers.

Adhering to these *Guiding Principles* will not be straightforward, easily accomplished, or inexpensive. To do so will require fundamental rethinking and restructuring of the relationships between the K-12 and higher education communities in SME&T, including financial relationships. It also will require fundamental revamping of teaching as a profession.

The committee also holds that a critical pathway to achieving these changes will be the establishment of K-16 partnerships whose integrated programs and activities go well beyond those of most partnerships that exist today.

The committee envisions that *all* of the contributors and stakeholders in these partnerships would be recognized and utilized for their professional expertise in science, mathematics, and technology education. The partners would work collectively toward improving teaching and ongoing professional development for *all teachers* in the partnership community, *including those in higher education*. These partnerships collectively would establish and implement goals for improving the learning and academic achievements in science, mathematics, and technology of students in affiliated institutions, including students in teacher education programs and the children in the schools that are members of the partnerships.

It is particularly critical for institutions that engage in partnerships to re-examine their traditional roles in teacher education and the ways in which what they do are financially supported. For example, colleges and universities traditionally have been involved in oversight of education for prospective teachers. However, these institutions actually may be better suited to overseeing the ongoing professional development of practicing teachers. Similarly, school personnel may be better able to organize, oversee, and mentor the practicum and internship phases of teacher education.

In these examples, funding for the various phases of the continuum of teacher education would need to be restructured. Specifically, the CSMTP envisions partnerships that are funded primarily through multi-year, line-item commitments in the budgets of the participating institutions. While gifts and grants from external funders enhance programs and opportunities for teachers, *they should not be the main source of support for collaborative partnerships for teacher education*. Even for colleges and universities that rely on tuition as a major source of institutional income, the CSMTP holds that supporting these partnerships will yield both explicit and less tangible benefits. In addition to the improved education that declared teacher candidates would receive from this arrangement, institutional participation in a partnership could open windows of opportunity for many other students who might be considering teaching as a career option; engagement in partnership activities might help them make a favorable decision. In addition, the service to and goodwill from the local community that a private institution could engender through its support of a partnership could be invaluable in promoting community relations.

The partnership model that the CSMTP envisions for improving teacher education and the profession of teaching is summarized in Figure 6-1 and described in detail in the next section.

FIGURE 6-1 A model for K-16 partnerships involving the people and resources critical to effective teacher education in science and mathematics. In this partnership model, scientists and mathematicians, teacher educators for science and mathematics, and mentor teachers work as equally essential partners to enhance teacher education and to promote more effective learning and curricular materials for students who attend the schools within the partnership. The members of the partnership also work together to facilitate professional growth and development for each other. The partnership's programs for teacher education ere informed by (1) educational research, (2) recommendations from national organizations involved with enhancing teaching, and (3) data gathered from the programs sponsored by the partnership itself.

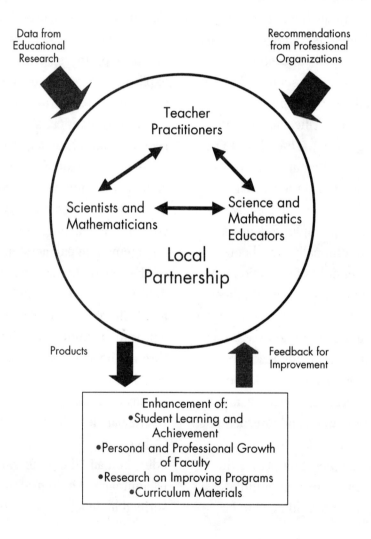

ARTICULATION OF THE COMMITTEE'S VISION FOR TEACHER EDUCATION

The strongest partnerships for teacher education would include, where possible, one or more school districts, two-year colleges, and four-year colleges and universities. Local businesses, industry, research laboratories, local or regional organizations, and individual scientists and mathematicians outside of academe also would be integral contributors to the design, planning, and implementation of these partnerships. Leaders at the highest levels from each of these sectors would need to demonstrate both to their institutions and to the larger community the importance they place on this kind of partnership.

As illustrated in Figure 6-1, teachers of science and mathematics in grades K-12, scientists and mathematicians, and science and mathematics teacher educators would serve as the core participants in this new type of partnership. Representatives from each of these groups who work together in this core would be selected on the basis of their expertise, interest, and commitment to improving teacher education. This core group would commit to developing a culture of recognition, respect, and trust that would give all partners equal voice and responsibility at the table.

Once the partnership was formed, its members would contribute both to the preparation of future educators and the improvement of the knowledge base and skills of *all* practicing teachers of science, mathematics, and technology in the K-12 *and* higher education sectors that are involved with the partnership. Implicit in this model is that, through their close professional association and interactions with master teachers from the partnership, scientists, mathematicians, engineers, and teacher educators at colleges and universities will have improved opportunities to enhance their own teaching skills. They also could increase their understanding of how students learn, and reexamine the scope, nature, and relevance of the content that they present in their courses.

New models for broadening the range of student teaching experiences and the planning and supervision of those experiences would be important work for the partnership. Similarly, the partnership would oversee the restructuring of continuing professional development for new and more experienced teachers employed by participating districts.

The policies and activities of the partnership would be informed by (1) educational research (both self-generated and from the scholarly literature—see below) that focuses on teachers, teaching, and curriculum and (2) recommendations for improving teacher education from national organizations (see Figure 3-1). Activities sponsored by the partnership also might include research involving teacher educators and teachers that explores ways to (1) implement and assess the efficacy of new approaches to teaching, curricula, and learning tools and (2) understand the systemic implications of implementing such changes (e.g., Confrey et al., in press). Partnerships that involve schools or districts and research universities could sponsor studies that focused on ways to improve teaching and learning of science, mathematics, and technology for people of all ages (e.g., AAU, 1999).

Perhaps most importantly, a partnership's programs for teacher education would be evaluated continually and modified when necessary. Ongoing feedback would come from two primary sources:

1. Evaluation of the science and mathematics activities in local schools and districts that participate in the partnership. Graduate students might undertake these evaluations as theses or district personnel or external evaluators could conduct such evaluations.

2. Collection of data about teachers who complete education and professional development programs sponsored by the partnership, as well as collection of data about the differences in levels of achievement of the students of those teachers.[1] Included would be student teachers who had moved to other parts of the state or country after graduation. Collection of such data would be a stimulus to colleges and universities to maintain contact with their graduates and to acknowledge the effectiveness of their teaching programs.

As illustrated in Figure 6-1, partnerships also would engage other resources in the community to contribute to planning and implementation of programs and to provide opportunities for future and practicing teachers to gain hands-on experience with local applications of science, mathematics, and technology. The community re-

[1]A number of colleges and universities, in collaboration with mentor teachers and district administrators, already monitor the success of their graduates who enter teaching. Examples include: Bank Street College, NY (see Wasley, 1999); The Beginning Teacher Support and Assessment Project – a two-year induction program established by the California Commission on Teacher Credentialing, that involves faculty from several California State University campuses, and personnel in school districts (Olebe et al., 1999); programs in Kentucky and Illinois that are similar to the California initiative also have been described (Brennan et al., 1999, and Heuser and Owens, 1999, respectively).

sources that could be tapped include businesses, industry, research laboratories, government agencies, and policymaking bodies.

The CSMTP wants to emphasize the critical need for *both* two- and four-year colleges to be core participants in partnerships and recipients of their value, whenever possible (see Figure 6-2). Recent data suggest that approximately 45 percent of the nation's undergraduates are enrolled in community colleges (and this percentage is likely to increase during the coming decade: American Association of Community Colleges, 2000). An increasingly high percentage of students may complete their entire undergraduate science and mathematics requirements in community colleges before transferring to four-year institutions to complete their baccalaureate degrees (NSF, 1998). Therefore, faculty in two-year institutions are very much needed to steer students toward additional courses in these subjects and to instill in students who will not go on to additional coursework an appreciation for the life and physical sciences, mathematics, and technology.

Efforts by two-year college faculty to recruit, educate, and support prospective teachers will be undermined, however, if those prospective teachers are not identified as such when they transfer to four-year institutions. Therefore, science and mathematics program planners at four-year colleges and universities need to work with their counterparts at community colleges to ensure appropriate course offerings for these students. Such planning could result in better integration and articulation of course offerings across the institutions, ensuring that prospective teachers receive a similar level of education in science and mathematics regardless of where they enroll in these courses. Community colleges and baccalaureate-granting institutions also should work together to ensure that general requirements for teacher education programs at the four-year institutions can be met by community college courses and that the credits are routinely transferable.

INSTITUTIONAL LEADERSHIP AND COMMITMENT

The presidents and chancellors of both the Association of American Universities (AAU, 1999) and the American Council on Education (ACE, 1999) have made strong statements that leaders of the nation's colleges and universities, and especially those with schools or colleges of education, need to affirm their institutions' commitments to teacher education and professional development as central priorities of their institutions. The CSMTP strongly

FIGURE 6-2 Organization of a partnership for teacher education showing the institutions that would contribute. The core of the partnership would be comprised of local school district(s) and two- and four-year colleges where possible. The partnership also would seek additional advice, expertise, and support from local and regional groups including business and industry, governmental and private funding sources, parent organizations, and other community agencies.

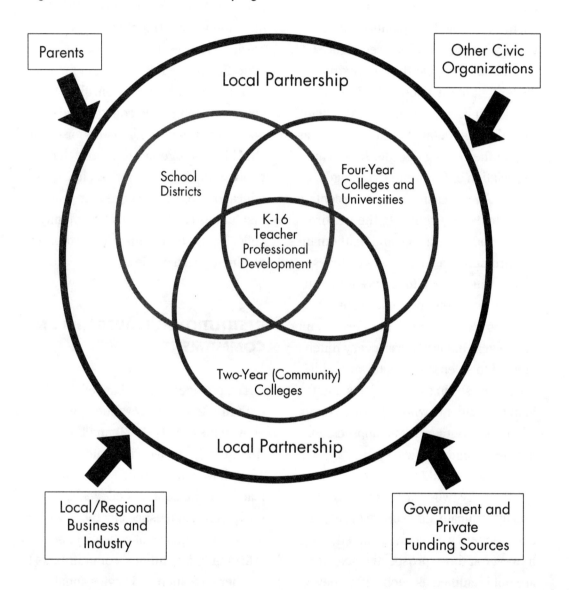

supports these declarations. Under the CSMTP's vision, college and university leaders would recognize the ramifications of real commitment to improving teacher education in science and mathematics. For example, faculty who teach lower division courses might need to restructure both content and pedagogical approaches, especially in courses that will be taken by prospective teachers for grades K-8, where many of these teachers will not become certified or endorsed in these subject areas. Many national organizations have called for *all* undergraduates to experience science and mathematics through inquiry-based approaches. This could require departments in these subject areas and their institutions to provide the facilities, equipment, and financial resources needed to give *all* students engaging laboratory and field experiences, including students who traditionally have not chosen such coursework in the past. In addition, postsecondary faculty members who teach such courses need tangible support and recognition for such efforts from their institution's leadership. These kinds of issues are discussed in greater detail in Chapter 7.

Depending on the structure of the partnership, leaders from the K-12 education community also must express their strong commitment to the success of the partnership. Under the CSMTP's vision, these leaders would affirm their schools' and districts' responsibility to provide funding for ongoing professional development of teachers and for designing a workplace environment that allows teachers to thrive as members of a professional community. In such an environment, time, tangible resources, and support would be provided to teachers for meaningful career enhancement activities. Teachers would have opportunities to work together and with their higher education counterparts to develop and evaluate programs. Both directly and through their participation

---

Once the relationship between the school and the college has been established, the teachers acquire leverage outside their classrooms and schools. The college connection enables teachers to redefine their roles and increase their responsibilities beyond the walls of their classrooms without leaving classroom teaching. . . . Teachers are provided with visibility and expand their professional influences and self-confidence, enabling them to assume "boundary-spanning" roles that none had experienced previously.

Boles and Troen, 1997

---

in the partnership, teachers' opinions and expertise would be sought for the most important policy decisions in schools and districts. The school workplace would encourage teachers to become leaders and mentors for their colleagues and reward them for doing so.

CHANGING ROLES FOR SCHOOLS, DISTRICTS, AND HIGHER EDUCATION IN TEACHER EDUCATION

The type of close-knit K-16 partnership proposed here offers new opportunities for districts and institutions of higher education to work together in ways that both extend and transcend their traditional roles in the education of science and mathematics teachers. The most common pattern of interaction has been for colleges and universities to take primary responsibility for preservice education and overseeing student teachers. Although classroom teachers may have more direct contact with student teachers or teacher interns, final responsibility for assigning grades and awarding certification usually has rested with institutions of higher education. Once students are graduated and certified, schools and districts then assume responsibility for induction programs and professional development. While colleges and universities may be better equipped to offer practicing teachers better opportunities to learn their subject matter more deeply and to engage in a more intellectual focus on education issues, few have formal agreements with school districts to do so.

Under the proposed partnership, this segregation of responsibilities could disappear, for the most part. Because scientists and mathematicians, teacher educators in these disciplines, and master/mentor teachers would work so closely together, all of them could be much more involved with every phase of teacher education and career development. Master classroom teachers could work together with college faculty in providing high-quality undergraduate courses that integrate content, pedagogy, and educational theory. At the same time, these courses could be more grounded in actual classroom practice and be offered at the sites where preservice students undertake their practicums and other student teaching experiences. Master teachers also could work with scientists and mathematicians who teach primarily content-based courses to help these college-level faculty members focus on appropriate content and better model effective classroom teaching. Improvement of pedagogy in undergraduate courses would benefit all students, majors and non-majors.

Close interaction among institutions also would allow preservice programs to vest greater responsibility for student teaching experiences in partner schools and districts. Contractual agreements would specify the level of service (e.g., direct supervision and mentoring) and interaction to be provided to students and also who would take responsibility for evaluations of student performance. These agreements also would specify the funding that each partner would commit—to support these and other endeavors of the partnership.

The partnerships envisioned here also would provide school districts with opportunities to improve their professional development programs in science, mathematics, and technology. In concert with their employing districts, teachers could earn academic credit and continuing education units at the two- and four-year colleges within their particular partnership or perhaps even within a system of connected partnerships whose teacher education programs are linked through information technology.

In contractual arrangements similar to those between higher education and industry, the institutions of higher education in partnerships could develop and offer ongoing, integrated professional development programs that are geared specifically to the needs of teachers of science, mathematics, and technology. Many college faculty have the expertise, facilities, and equipment necessary to offer to practicing teachers the kinds of higher level courses that they need to gain much deeper knowledge and understanding of the subject matter they teach. Experienced teachers are likely to be ready for such courses; i.e., more motivated and better prepared through their classroom experiences to learn about more abstract issues, such as theories of learning and cognition. Some combination of faculty from the life and physical sciences, schools of education, and master teachers could stimulate levels of professional and intellectual growth that would be nearly impossible for achieve from other, similar programs offered only by districts or institutions of higher education alone.

Partnerships also could work with their state's department of education to find ways to offer appropriate academic credit to teachers who upgrade their content knowledge and instructional skills in science, mathematics, or technology. The awarding of appropriate academic credit is particularly important for teachers who may not have specific teaching credentials in science, mathematics, and technology but who are expected to teach these subjects anyway (e.g., many teachers of the elementary and middle grades). For these teachers, undergraduate-level courses in science, mathematics, or engineering may be most appropriate.

However, because these teachers already have earned bachelors degrees, some states will not permit them to receive continuing education credits by enrolling in undergraduate courses. Graduate-level courses could be seen as a solution; however, as currently offered, they may not provide teachers with the kind of education and professional development that would best serve their needs. The integrated programs that partnerships could develop and offer to experienced teachers might address the problem not only by offering appropriate courses to teachers but also by assuaging official concerns about whether the credits they would obtain would reflect appropriate academic levels of study.

Teachers in the partnership districts also could engage in research projects in their disciplines by working with college faculty who are involved with the partnership or with undergraduate or graduate students who are engaged in disciplinary or interdisciplinary research. Teachers also could have increased opportunities to undertake research related to the improvement of science, mathematics, or technology education. For example, the partnership could arrange for undergraduate students to work with children in the partnership schools and also establish ways for teachers to share scientific equipment, computing facilities and software, mathematical manipulatives, and other resources owned by the higher education partners. In some cases, college faculty also could benefit by using equipment, such as mathematical manipulatives, that may be more commonly found in the K-12 schools in the partnership. A portion of the funding dedicated to the partnership would need to be set aside to provide teacher participants in this research from both the K-12 and higher education partner institutions with sufficient time to plan, work with undergraduate or graduate students, and evaluate the efficacy of their work.

Clearly, as outlined above, new approaches to and sources of funding would be needed for this model of teacher education. Such funds could be realized from several sources, including those normally set aside by school districts for inservice training of teachers, although, in some school districts, the amount of funds set aside might need to be increased, in recognition of the importance of professional development. Support could be sought from locally based businesses and industries that have publicly acknowledged the importance of science, mathematics, and technology education and possibly even funded such improvements in the past. Support also could be sought from state and federal agencies through existing grant programs (e.g., the

Eisenhower Act for Improving Science and Mathematics Education[2] or Teacher Enhancement grants from the National Science Foundation[3]).

Because the professional development of teachers should parallel the development programs that support people in other professions, the employers of teachers should view ongoing professional development enhancement as a core component of their commitment to their employees. This commitment must include adequate financial support. *Financial support from school districts should be an integral component of any budget created for partnerships. The CSMTP emphasizes that, as professionals, teachers should not be expected to pay for programs that are professionally mandated. Rather, given the accumulating body of compelling evidence that student achievement is directly tied to the level of teachers' knowledge of subject matter and appropriate ways to teach it, districts must view ongoing, high-quality professional development programs for teachers as a critical investment for improving student learning.*

OTHER BENEFITS OF PARTNERSHIPS FOR TEACHER EDUCATION IN SCIENCE AND MATHEMATICS

In addition to making more seamless teacher education programs possible, carefully and thoughtfully designed partnerships can provide numerous other benefits to the people and institutions. These include

1. Coordination of efforts to recruit students to science and mathematics teaching. For science and mathematics, teacher shortages appear to be localized, at least at the moment (Darling-Hammond, personal communication with the committee). In addition, Feistritzer et al. (1999b) have presented data suggesting that, unlike many other professionals, new K-12 teachers are likely to find teaching positions close to where they lived before entering college or near the universities where they were educated. This suggests that, through a coordinated effort, partnerships involving local school districts could be especially effective in attracting graduates of local

---

[2]Additional information about Eisenhower funds is available at <http://www.ed.gov/legislation/ ESEA/compliance/eisen.html>. Note that when this report was being prepared for publication, the U.S. Congress had been debating whether to maintain Eisenhower funds for professional development of teachers exclusively in science and mathematics or to make the funds more widely available to professional development in other subject areas.

[3]Additional information about this program is available at < http://www.ehr.nsf.gov/ehr/esie/ TE.htm>.

high schools to teaching. It is not unreasonable to expect that students of schools participating in partnerships would already have experienced the kinds of teaching that would lay the groundwork for them to go on to become effective teachers themselves. The coordinated teacher education programs provided by the partnerships envisioned here would assist these students in becoming particularly well-qualified teacher candidates.

In addition, through programs and incentives, partnerships could become important catalysts that encouraged high-achieving local students to consider careers teaching science, mathematics, or technology. For example, the partnerships could provide opportunities for local students to interact closely with student and mentor teachers who are involved with the partnership. Partnerships could offer opportunities for prospective teacher candidates to visit and participate in university-sponsored recruiting programs during the school year, on weekends, or during summers. The partnerships also could create a coordinated system of advising that spans the high school and college years to encourage more students to consider teaching as a career.

2. Availability of student teachers and interns. Establishing a formal agreement that makes student teachers and interns available to partner school districts would give these districts ready access to the pool of preservice teachers who are enrolled in the two- and four-year colleges and universities within the partnership. Because all of the parties would have agreed on standards for preservice preparation in science, mathematics, and technology as well as in pedagogy, districts could be assured that these preservice students would be qualified to undertake a practicum, internship, or other teaching experience. In turn, institutions of higher education could be confident that the students they sent out as student teachers would have a teaching experience of high quality, assisted by the district's own experienced teachers in consultation with the students' college or university supervisors.

An impediment to this plan is the need for financial support. Many potential teacher candidates, especially those from lower socioeconomic or underrepresented populations, cannot afford to spend extended periods of time in practicums or other kinds of student teaching due to family and other financial obligations. Financial support of potential teachers would enable a more diverse population to consider teaching as a profession.

3. Definition and enforcement of standards of quality for teacher preparation and professional development, including routes for certifi-

cation of science and mathematics teachers. Enforced standards are critical components of effective teacher education. In partnerships, both higher education institution and school partners need to develop mutually acceptable goals and objectives for the programs in which they are engaged and to do what is necessary to ensure that those goals are met. Through contractual agreements and close interaction, the members of the partnership could establish comprehensive expectations and standards both for the providers and the "consumers" of teacher education programs. These expectations could extend well beyond education courses and student teaching experiences. For example, the partnership could work to establish how to make science and mathematics courses for prospective and practicing teachers more relevant and taught more effectively at the partnership's member colleges and universities.

In addition, by clearly defining what constitutes appropriate credentials for prospective teachers before they begin their student teaching experiences, districts would be assured that these student teachers would be able to handle the challenges that await them in the classroom. Because partnerships as envisioned here also would be able to design and undertake educational research projects that measure and

analyze the learning and achievement of the K-12 students being taught, all of the partners would learn how their contributions and efforts for improving practicums and other field experiences for student teachers might be revised or strengthened.

Establishing such credentials for high-quality teaching also might assist those who take non-partnership or nontraditional paths to becoming teachers. For example, students who have graduated from colleges outside the partnership or people who have the requisite knowledge and skills in science and mathematics but who have not taken formal education courses might be able to become teachers in the partnership. At least on a provisional basis, these students could participate in internships and other kinds of professional development on their way to earning full certification. These types of standards and opportunities might have the added benefit of allowing a district to continue to diversify its teaching force.

4. Opportunities for ongoing, informal professional development. One component of the crisis in science and mathematics education is that professionals who work in the cultures of K-12 and higher education rarely know about or understand what takes place in each other's work environment. Partnerships can provide both formal and informal opportunities to end this isolation. For example, science and mathematics departments and schools of education typically offer a number of guest lectures, films, debates, and other presentations during the academic year but, typically, teachers do not know about them. The partnership could amend that by making a special effort to inform and invite teachers to such events. The partnership also could arrange participation by teachers in afternoon and weekend field trips and other course-related activities offered by science and mathematics faculty or departments. In turn, schools could target college faculty to participate in various activities and events within their purview. These might include science fairs, where scientists, mathematicians, and engineers are usually needed to serve as judges, the development of nature preserves near partnership schools to allow children to collect and analyze scientific data, or participation in textbook selection or grant-writing teams. Perhaps most importantly, the establishment of partnerships also would make it easier for college faculty, especially those in science, mathematics, and engineering, to visit partnership schools and actually observe what happens in classrooms. These visits could help college-level faculty better understand the kind and level of content being taught in partner schools, allow

them to have more informed input to the partnership about that content, and influence their own teaching methods.

5. Enhanced professionalism for teachers. Because teachers are equal partners at the table and critical contributors to the success of the partnership endeavor, teaching as a profession would take on more of the characteristics of other professions. When teachers are required to articulate their ideas, to express clearly what they do in their classrooms and why they do it, and to share their ideas openly with peers and other professional colleagues, their teaching is likely to be enhanced. As teachers become more involved with various kinds of scientific or educational research, they go beyond their traditional roles by helping to discover new knowledge that can then be applied directly to their own classrooms and to the classrooms of colleagues associated with and beyond the partnership. Vesting such responsibilities and authority in teachers results in greater ownership and understanding of teaching as a profession.

Teachers will need time and financial as well as other resources (e.g., availability of qualified substitute teachers, aides) to be full contributors in any partnership. For the partnership to have such a level of contribution from teachers—and to enable teachers to grow as professionals in the process—

school districts will need to work with their partners to find ways to provide the time and resources required. Providing this time implies that (1) teachers will have fewer contact hours with students each day or week, (2) they will be engaged in (and fully compensated for) their work for a longer period of time each academic year (e.g., by working an extra month during the summers on professional and curriculum development), or (3) some combination of these options. The critical components of a teaching position that could be supported in these ways include professional reflection, continual intellectual engagement, and advancement in the profession (e.g., Figure 6-4), working with colleagues to improve specific curricula, and working with each other and with less senior teachers to improve teaching and learning for all of the schools involved with the partnership (e.g., Ma, 1999). Providing opportunities and the financial support that is required for teachers to become more fully engaged in their profession throughout the academic year is common practice in other nations such as Japan (Stigler and Hiebert, 1997; NRC, 1999c).

6. Sharing of resources and expertise. With few exceptions, colleges and universities in a given geographical area are far more likely than local school districts to have sophisticated laboratory space and equipment, computing facilities, and access to other resources such as library holdings. As partnerships for teacher education in science and mathematics develop and prioritize their issues, sharing of knowledge and resources could become a primary focus. In terms of technology and technology applications knowledge, for example, recent reports (Becker and Anderson, 1998; Milken Family Foundation, 1999; CEO Forum, 1999, 2000; Brandt, 2000) have decried the lack of preparation of future teachers in the appropriate use of information technology, as well as the continued need for practicing teachers to work to incorporate general purpose technology tools into core instructional activities. Because of their familiarity and comfort with using sophisticated information technology tools and software, scientists and mathematicians from the partnership and their expertise could be engaged to address these issues more fully. In turn, these scientists and mathematicians also could apply their experiences from such efforts to address appropriate applications of information technology in undergraduate classrooms and laboratories for a wider spectrum of students.

In terms of equipment resources, members in a partnership might decide that certain kinds of expensive instrumentation and equipment would be useful both in high school and introductory college laboratories. The existence of the partnership could then open the door to the sharing of current equipment or the pooling of funds to jointly purchase new equipment, with obvious cost savings benefits. More efficient use of the equipment over the academic year and during the summers might also be arranged.

FINANCIAL SUPPORT FOR PARTNERSHIPS FOR TEACHER EDUCATION

The kind of partnership program described here should be viewed as a model that can be adapted to local or regional situations: therefore, estimating precise costs of establishing, operating, and sustaining such an effort is not possible. However, the committee's vision—that institutions of higher education and school districts share responsibility for all phases of teacher education and professional development—also must extend to the ways in which partnerships are supported financially. Accordingly, the CSMTP suggests that funds previously devoted by individual organizations to their current programs in teacher education be pooled within the partnership. Through contractual agreements, the respective

partner organizations would authorize the partnership to spend these funds as needed to provide a continuum of support of teacher education.

Under this plan, it is entirely possible that funds which colleges and universities would otherwise expend to support their own student teacher programs might be used instead by school districts, if the partnership determined that districts should assume primary responsibility for this phase of teacher education. Some of these funds might be used by the partnership to support mentor teachers who would work with university faculty members to teach preservice courses. Likewise, school district funds previously used to support district professional development programs might instead be transferred to institutions of higher education within the partnership to support continuing professional development programs.

By combining these separate line items from the various partners, the partnership could enjoy flexibility in deciding how to develop its programs. By pooling such funds, the partnership also could then determine whether additional funds are required. Those funds could then be sought from a variety of sources, including school boards, deans or provosts, local, state, and federal government agencies, or private sources. Once a partnership had a coordinated policy for teacher education and a pool of funds to support it, the partnership could more easily justify the need for additional funds. As always, the argument for expending any funds for the partnership's efforts at any time would be to support more effective teacher education programs.

An important consideration in this approach to teacher education in science and mathematics would be the reduction or possibly even the elimination of redundancy of effort, programs, and equipment. Although formal financial analyses would be required for each partnership, CSMTP members predict that the sponsoring organizations either would actually save money or obtain more services than would be possible if each organization continued to operate its own programs divorced from the activities and priorities of others.

POTENTIAL OBSTACLES TO SUSTAINING AN EFFECTIVE PARTNERSHIP FOR TEACHER EDUCATION

Leaders both within the core of a partnership and in the institutions that support it must recognize and attempt to mitigate the many external variables that could compromise the success and vitality of the partnership (see Figure 6-3). For example,

• Current **tenure and promotion policies** at many colleges and universities may not sufficiently recognize the contributions of faculty in science, mathematics, engineering, *and* in education departments to the improvement of teacher education through such partnerships (e.g., NRC, 1999h). In many cases, these kinds of partnership activities require more commitment of time, effort, and intellectual engagement than other, more traditional faculty responsibilities. If institutions and faculty colleagues who are not engaged in such activities do not recognize and reward such efforts, partnerships are not likely to be sustained over time.

• **Sufficient funding** for successful partnerships must be both predictable and available long-term. Budgets that are subject to annual negotiation can have a negative impact on this kind of compact. Partnerships that depend too heavily on grants rather than on line items in the budgets of school districts and postsecondary institutions can be compromised if the priorities of funding agencies shift over time.

• Real **buy-in** by a partner institution has ramifications for the entire institution. Partnerships cannot be optimally effective if one or more partners are unwilling or unable to meet their commitments. **Contractual agreements** must be equitable and supported financially through line items in the budgets

FIGURE 6-3 In the system of gears illustrated above, the large main gear and all of the components with which it meshes must be working synchronously for the system to operate. A malfunction in any one of the smaller gears can cause the entire system to malfunction. Like a system of gears, local partnerships are subject to a variety of external influences. Individually or in combination, these external influences can provide opportunities to move the partnership forward or they can bring the system to a halt, even when other components of the system are functioning properly. Several kinds of external influences on K-16 partnerships are illustrated. Those responsible for such partnerships must understand how external factors can influence their operation.

of all parties that are involved with the partnership.

• As noted before (and in Figure 6-4), the kind of partnership the committee envisions would allow people with appropriate experience and expertise to pursue teaching careers through non-traditional routes to the profession. However, state departments of educa-tion or accreditation bodies would need to be involved with this type of opportu-nity through the creation of policies that enable prospective teachers (both traditional undergraduate candidates and those who pursue teaching later in their careers through alternative path-ways) to earn **certification through the partnership**.

FIGURE 6-4 The continuum of teacher professional development. In this model, teachers have the opportunities for continued professional growth throughout their careers. They also have the opportunity to assume leadership roles in their schools, in partnerships with local colleges and universities, and through leadership in their district, state, and nationally. These experiences, in turn, contribute to further opportu-nities for individual professional growth and development.

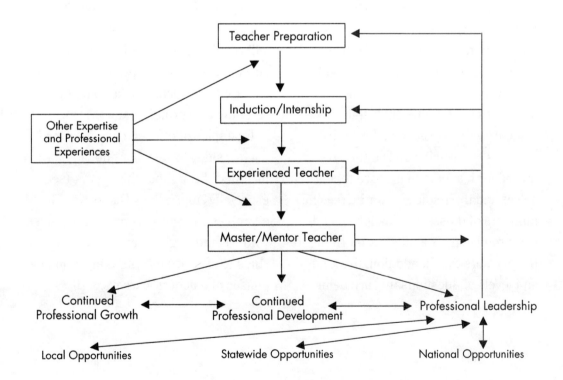

• Most of the people connected with the kind of partnership envisioned here also would likely have academic and **other responsibilities to their home institutions**, which, like most jobs in education, might also be more than full time. Unless these contributors are provided with sufficient time and support to engage in the partnership, responsibility for it will probably fall on the shoulders of only a few. To prevent the destructive tensions such a situation can easily generate, all institutions that contribute to a partnership should consider some redefinition of contributors' jobs to give them the time needed to be true collaborators.

• The partnerships envisioned here call for new approaches to teaching and assessment of teaching and student learning. Many of the ideas espoused in the committee's vision for improving teaching and learning may be at odds with current efforts in some districts and states to institute "high-stakes" standardized assessments for both students and teachers. The time required for teachers to prepare themselves and their students for increasing numbers of these examinations could compromise their ability to contribute to the partnership. In addition, the kinds and levels of questions that are being used in some of these tests (e.g., emphasis on facts and information vs. conceptual understanding) could undermine the kinds of teaching that the committee envisions would result as a result of the teacher education within these partnerships.

Finally, and perhaps most importantly, the committee acknowledges that achieving this vision will not be straightforward or easily accomplished. It will require fundamental rethinking and restructuring of the relationships between the K-12 and higher education communities in science, mathematics, engineering, and technology, including financial relationships. Building the kind of capacity that is needed to begin or to grow a partnership for teacher education as envisioned in this report will require a great deal of time and commitment from all parties. It also will require fundamental revamping of teaching as a profession.

Examples of efforts to work toward partnerships for teacher education are included throughout this report (see especially Appendixes D and E). These examples can serve as models for those who wish to begin or expand partnerships to improve teacher education at all phases of teachers' careers.

7
Recommendations

GENERAL RECOMMENDATIONS

The Committee on Science and Mathematics Teacher Preparation recommends that

1. **Teacher education in science, mathematics, and technology be viewed as a continuum of programs and professional experiences that enables individuals to move seamlessly from college preparation for teaching to careers in teaching these subject areas;**

2. **Teacher education be viewed as a career-long process that allows teachers of science, mathematics, and technology to acquire and regularly update the content knowledge and pedagogical tools needed to teach in ways that enhance student learning and achievement in these subjects; and**

3. **Teacher education also be structured in ways that allow teachers to grow individually in their profession and to contribute to the further enhancement of both teaching and their disciplines.**

As outlined, then detailed in its vision in Chapter 6, the Committee on Science and Mathematics Teacher Preparation (CSMTP) believes that the goals and objectives of the general recommendations given above can be achieved by all two- and four-year colleges and universities (those with and without programs in teacher education) working with school districts to establish partnerships for teacher education.

In addition, in this chapter, the CSMTP also offers more specific recommendations in the areas of (1) recruitment and preparation of new teachers (preservice education), (2) the induction of new teachers for their first teaching positions, and (3) continuing professional development (inservice) for practicing teachers of science, mathematics, and technology. Consistent with the committee's vision of making teacher preparation and professional development a seamless continuum, the committee's specific recommendations for each of these stages in the professional lives of teachers are woven into a continuum framework. The intended audiences for each recommendation are indicated by **boldface** type. All of the committee's specific recommendations are listed first in Table 7-1, then detailed below.

RECOMMENDATIONS FOR GOVERNMENTS

Local, state, and federal governments should recognize and acknowledge the need to improve teacher education in science and mathematics, as well as assist the public in understanding and supporting improvement.

Governments should understand that restructuring teacher education will require large infusions of financial support and make a strong commitment to provide the direct and indirect funding required to support local and regional partnerships for improving

Almost 10 years ago, President Bush and the state governors set goals aimed at preparing all the Nation's children to improve their achievement in core subjects and outpace the world in at least math and science by 2000. . . . The urgency of the ensuing national debate on how to improve academic achievement by U.S. elementary-, middle-, and high school students—and the consequences of failing to do so—remains undiminished today. At issue is who ostensibly defines the content to be learned, and who ensures the opportunity to teach and learn it well. While resolutions will be local, the dialogue that precedes them should reflect experiences from across the Nation, as well as research and evaluation of processes and outcomes, including international comparisons.

National Science Board, 1999, page 1

teacher education in these disciplines. They also should encourage the recruitment and retention of teachers of science and mathematics through

- low-interest student loans,
- loan forgiveness for recently

TABLE 7-1 Specific Recommendations

FOR GOVERNMENTS

Local, state, and federal governments should recognize and acknowledge the need to improve teacher education in science and mathematics, as well as assist the public in understanding and supporting improvement. Governments should understand that restructuring teacher education will require large infusions of financial support and make a strong commitment to provide the direct and indirect funding required to support local and regional partnerships for improving teacher education in these disciplines. They also should encourage the recruitment and retention of teachers of science and mathematics—particularly those who are qualified "in-field"—through financial incentives, such as salaries that are commensurate and competitive with other professions in science, mathematics, and technology; low-interest student loans; loan forgiveness for recently certified teachers in these disciplines who commit to teaching; stipends for teaching internships; and grants to teachers, school districts, or teacher education partnerships to offset the costs of continual professional development.

FOR COLLABORATION BETWEEN INSTITUTIONS OF HIGHER EDUCATION AND THE K-12 COMMUNITY

Two- and four-year institutions of higher education and school districts that are involved with partnerships for teacher education should—working together—establish a comprehensive, integrated system of recruiting and advising people who are interested in teaching science, mathematics, and technology.

FOR THE HIGHER EDUCATION COMMUNITY

1. Science, mathematics, and engineering departments at two- and four-year colleges and universities should assume greater responsibility for offering college-level courses that provide teachers with strong exposure to appropriate content and that model the kinds of pedagogical approaches appropriate for teaching that content.

2. Two- and four-year colleges and universities should reexamine and redesign introductory college-level courses in science and mathematics to better accommodate the needs of practicing and future teachers.

3. Universities whose primary mission includes education research should set as a priority the development and execution of peer-reviewed research studies that focus on ways to improve teacher education, the art of teaching, and learning for people of all ages. New research that focuses broadly on synthesizing data across studies and linking it to school practice in a wide variety of school settings would be especially helpful to the improvement of teacher education and professional development for both prospective and experienced teachers. The results of this research should be collated and disseminated through a national electronic database or library.

continued

TABLE 7-1 Continued

4. Two- and four-year colleges and universities should maintain contact with and provide guidance to teachers who complete their preparation and development programs.

5. Following a period of collaborative planning and preparation, **two- and four-year colleges and universities** in a partnership for teacher education should assume primary responsibility for providing professional development opportunities to experienced teachers of science, mathematics, and technology. Such programs would involve faculty from science, mathematics, and engineering disciplines and from schools of education.

FOR THE K-12 EDUCATION COMMUNITY

1. Following a period of collaborative planning and preparation, **school districts** in a partnership for teacher education should assume primary responsibility for providing high-quality *practicum* experiences and internships for prospective teachers.

2. School districts in a partnership for teacher education should assume primary responsibility for developing and overseeing field experiences, student teaching, and internship programs for new teachers of science, mathematics, and technology.

3. School districts should collaborate with **two- and four-year colleges and universities** to provide professional development opportunities to experienced teachers of science, mathematics, and technology. Such programs would involve faculty from science, mathematics, and engineering disciplines and from schools of education. Teachers who participate in these programs would, in turn, offer their expertise and guidance to others involved with the partnership.

FOR PROFESSIONAL AND DISCIPLINARY ORGANIZATIONS

1. Organizations that represent institutions of higher education should assist their members in establishing programs to help new teachers. For example, databases of information about new teachers would be developed and shared among member institutions so that colleges and universities could be notified when a newly certified teacher was moving to their area to teach. Those colleges and universities could then plan and offer welcoming and support activities, such as opportunities for continued professional and intellectual growth.

2. Professional disciplinary societies in science, mathematics, and engineering, higher education organizations, governments at all levels, and business and industry should become more engaged partners (as opposed to advisors or overseers) in efforts to improve teacher education.

3. Professional disciplinary societies in science, mathematics, and engineering, and higher education organizations also should work together to align their policies and recommendations for improving teacher education in science, mathematics, and engineering.

certified teachers in these disciplines who commit to teaching for at least three years,

• additional loan forgiveness for teachers of science, mathematics, and technology who agree to teach in schools with high levels of poverty or low levels of student achievement in these subject areas,

• stipends for teaching internships,

• grants to teachers, school districts, or teacher education partnerships to offset the costs of ongoing professional development in these subject areas.

Most importantly, if teachers are to be held to higher levels of professional accountability, ways must be found to provide them with levels of compensation and working conditions that are competitive with other professions that recruit people with the kinds of credentials held by teachers of science and mathematics and that are commensurate with the experiences of other professionals with similar levels of education and training (see U.S. Department of Education, 1999). The problem is especially acute for people with backgrounds in science, mathematics, and technology. In today's economy, it is much easier and more lucrative for almost anyone with a background in engineering, technology, science, or mathematics to find desirable levels of salary, benefits, and working conditions

in other sectors. If governments continue to expect increasing levels of performance and accountability both for teachers and their students, then they also must provide both the compensation and the kinds of professional workplace and working conditions that would allow higher standards to be realized. Indeed, it may be necessary to provide higher levels of compensation to teachers of mathematics, science, and technology to recruit and retain the best teachers to these disciplines (see Odden and Kelley, 1997; North Central Regional Educational Laboratory, 1999; Olson, 1999; Kelley et al., 2000; and Odden, 2000).

The federal government also should examine ways to provide assistance with improving the teaching of science, mathematics, and technology in ways that local and state governments cannot do individually. These initiatives could include

• **Setting aside funds for ongoing professional development for teachers of science, mathematics, and technology.** The committee strongly recommends that Eisenhower Grant funds continue to be restricted to professional development in science and mathematics. As the U.S. Congress considers reauthorization of the Elementary and Secondary Education Act, there have been attempts to make the Eisenhower Grants less restrictive.

Given the critical need for improving science and mathematics education in the United States, the CSMTP opposes any attempt to make these very limited funds available for other purposes. However, a suitable compromise would be to allow some portion of these funds to be made available to teachers from other disciplines who wish to become more knowledgeable about science, mathematics, and technology. For example, a history or social studies teacher who would like to understand more about how science and technology have influenced society in this country or other parts of the world should be able to use Eisenhower funds to learn about such issues.

• **Providing funding that would enable prospective and practicing teachers who otherwise would be unable to benefit from participating in a partnership to do so.** The CSMTP recommends that the partnership opportunities described in Chapter 6 be extended to as many prospective and experienced teachers as possible. For those schools and districts that are located too far from institutions of higher education to form their own partnerships, government funds should be made available that would enable teachers from these districts to benefit

from existing partnerships in a nearby locale. Such support could include the establishment of electronic links that would enable practicing teachers to engage in high-quality professional development activities and stipends that would allow either prospective or practicing teachers to undertake extended internships with an existing partnership.

• **Establishing a national database for improving teaching of science, mathematics, and technology.** Nearly every state is at some stage of developing databases and other resources for its teachers to enable them to understand and teach to state standards in science and mathematics. While every state's standards differ to some degree, most of them are based at least in part on the national standards for science and mathematics. Thus, it is likely that great deal of overlapping effort is taking place. If the federal government could establish a national database for improving the teaching of science, mathematics, and technology that would allow teachers to easily access information from their state and elsewhere, teaching of these disciplines could be vastly improved (e.g., NRC, 1998, 1999g). The National Science Foundation's National Digital Library project[1] could serve as the focal point

---

[1]The National Science, Mathematics, Engineering, and Technology Education Digital Library program will be a network of learning environments and resources for science, mathematics, engineering, and technology education. The library will ultimately meet the needs of students and teachers at

for such a compendium of information. The CSMTP recommends that future Requests for Proposals include specific requests to develop this national database and library on teaching of science, mathematics, and technology.

• **Creating a national database that lists job openings and teacher candidates for science, mathematics, and technology.** As indicated elsewhere in this report, there is great variance in both the supply of and demand for qualified teachers across the country. A national registry that lists available positions and the names and résumés of teacher candidates who are seeking positions might greatly reduce the overabundance of teachers in some parts of the country and the critical shortages of teachers in others. The U.S. Department of Education could oversee this registry or it could become part of the NSF's National Digital Library for Science, Mathematics, Engineering, and Technology Education, once that library is established.

• **Developing national consensus on criteria for teacher credentialing.** The CSMTP recommends that the U.S. Secretary of Education convene a panel of representatives from the 50 states for the purpose of reaching consensus on a set of uniform criteria for teacher credentialing that would allow teachers of science, mathematics, and technology who earn certification in one state to teach in any other.

The CSMTP envisions that the development of such consensus criteria would be based on high standards for teaching and also would be valid in all states for some agreed upon number of years. Each state also would be able to reserve the right to require some additional number of hours of credit for specific coursework in that state (e.g., courses on state history). Teachers who received a credential under this agreement would be required to take these additional courses prior to obtaining their first re-certification in that state.

all levels—K-12, undergraduate, graduate, and lifelong learning—in both individual and collaborative settings. It will serve not only as a gateway to a rich array of current and future high-quality educational content and services but also as a forum where resource users may become resource providers. For example, users might contribute their expertise to produce new teaching modules from resources such as real-time experimental data or visualization software available through the network. Or they might evaluate and report on the efficacy of specific digital learning objects (such as Java applets or interactive electronic notebooks) and their impact on student learning. Beyond providing traditional library functions, such as the intelligent retrieval of relevant information, indexing and online annotation of resources, and archiving of materials, the digital library will also enable users to access virtual collaborative work areas, hands-on laboratory experiences, tools for analysis and visualization, remote instruments, large databases of real-time or archived data, simulated or virtual environments, and other new capabilities as they emerge (NSF, 2000).

Coupled with the development of a national registry for teacher positions and available candidates, this national consensus on teacher certification could help ease regional shortages of teachers and lead to greater agreement about what teachers of science, mathematics, and technology should know and be able to do.

RECOMMENDATIONS FOR COLLABORATION BETWEEN INSTITUTIONS OF HIGHER EDUCATION AND THE K-12 COMMUNITY

Two- and four-year institutions of higher education and school districts that are involved with partnerships for teacher education should establish a comprehensive, integrated system of recruiting and advising people who are interested in teaching science, mathematics, and technology.

The members of the CSMTP are convinced that the recruitment of high-quality teachers in science, mathematics, and technology is truly a national need and must become a national priority. Colleges and universities must contribute to attracting the best and brightest candidates to the profession. Efforts to attract the best students to science, mathematics, and technology teaching should be of a magnitude similar to efforts now used to recruit students to other professions, such as medicine, law, and graduate programs in the natural sciences and engineering. Science, mathematics, and engineering departments should be active participants with their institutions in the recruitment and ongoing support of students who have indicated their interest in pursuing careers in teaching. Their institutions should recognize departments that are especially effective in these efforts.

Departments or colleges of science, mathematics, engineering and technology at two- and four-year colleges and universities that offer teacher education programs also should provide services to prospective teachers at levels that are comparable to those offered to students who plan to pursue careers in other professions in the life and physical sciences, mathematics, and engineering. These services should include the appointment of a pre-teaching advisor or an advisory committee. These advisors would be given the time and resources required to establish programs for recruiting students who are interested in science, mathematics, and engineering and who also relate well to children and young adults at the elementary or secondary levels. They also would advise these students on issues and options for becoming certified teachers. Advisors would work with their departmental colleagues, faculty in the institution's school of education, and with local schools involved with a partnership. These advisors either should be suitably compensated for their work or provided with sufficient amounts of released time from other responsibilities to carry out this work. In addition, the quality of advising should be taken into account during personnel decisions. The advisor or advising group also would have primary responsibility for coordinating the campus' teacher preparation efforts with those of community colleges that are sending large numbers of students to the campus (see Recommendations for the Higher Education Community, Recommendation 3).

Colleges and universities that do not provide formal teacher education programs should recognize that prospective teachers of science, mathematics, and technology also matriculate on their campuses. At a minimum, faculty advisors should be designated in these disciplines. These advisors should learn about the procedures for credentialing in their state, alternative routes to certification, and the challenges and opportunities that K-12 teachers face so that they can offer appropriate advice and guidance to these students.

However, postsecondary faculty in the sciences, mathematics, engineering, and technology should not delegate all responsibility for advising and mentoring future teachers to a specified advisor or advisory committee. Job descriptions for new faculty hires or redefinitions of responsibilities for continuing faculty who teach and advise undergraduate students should include the expectation that applicants have or are willing to acquire the knowledge they will need to help students learn about careers in teaching.

Through their words, actions, and financial support, the highest level administrators should reaffirm or indicate that pre-teaching advisors or advisory committees will be integral components of the institution's academic and career support programs (ACE, 1999). Again, the CSMTP concurs with the conclusions of others (e.g., ACE, 1999; NRC, 1999h) that teacher education must become a campus-wide priority, not solely the purview of departments or colleges of education. If such commitments cannot be made and sustained, continuation of formal programs for teacher preparation and professional development on those campuses should be called into question.

RECOMMENDATIONS FOR THE HIGHER EDUCATION COMMUNITY

1. Science, mathematics, and engineering departments at two- and four-year colleges and universities should assume greater responsibility for offering college-level courses that provide teachers with strong exposure to appropriate content and that model the kinds of pedagogical approaches appropriate for teaching that content.

Postsecondary institutions that educate teachers of science and mathematics should articulate clear connections between their programs and the high standards that national professional organizations have established for beginning and more experienced teachers. These connections could be formulated by the partnership for teacher education to which the postsecondary institutions belong and could then be used to guide the development and improvement of teacher education programs.

Science and mathematics courses for preservice teachers should be rich in appropriate content. Courses should offer fewer topics and allow students to explore the topics presented in greater depth. Content offered in science and mathematics courses for prospective teachers should be presented in ways that teachers can adapt to their own classrooms. In addition, the teaching of effective pedagogy should not be delegated to education courses. College and university faculty in the SME&T disciplines who offer courses for prospective teachers should model effective teaching techniques through their own classroom practices. In partnerships, K-12 classroom teachers who have strong pedagogical knowledge and skills could help their higher education counterparts model such approaches to teaching.

Other organizations have attempted to define preparation for teachers of science and mathematics in terms of subjects to be covered and amount of exposure to various disciplines. For example, a recent report from the Learning First Alliance (1998) recommends specific content knowledge that middle-school specialists in mathematics should acquire. The Alliance also calls for teachers of middle-grades mathematics to be familiar with all of the mathematics taught in grades K-12, with special emphasis on the grade below and the grade above the teacher's own. The National Science Teachers Association (1998) has prepared similar criteria for teachers of science.

However, as the aforementioned organizations and others also emphasize, well-prepared teachers must have a deep knowledge and understanding of their discipline and of effective pedagogy, as well as the capacity to use pedagogical content knowledge to influence student learning. Research shows that students demonstrate higher levels of achievement when they learn from teachers who are well versed in their subject areas (e.g., see Chapter 3). A critical component of such competence comes from deep knowledge and understanding, as compared to memorization, of the subjects that teachers present to their students (Shulman, 1986; Coble and Koballa, 1996; Manouchehri, 1997; and Grouws and Schultz, 1996).

An expanding body of research is now exploring what content teachers of science and mathematics should know and how they can best acquire such knowledge (NRC, 2000b; Ma, 1999). Although experts have not yet reached consensus on a core body of knowledge that every teacher should know to be able to teach at a given grade level, they agree that how teachers come to understand content knowledge in their disciplines is as important as the specific information they learn.

College and university scientists, mathematicians, and engineers should emphasize conceptual understanding of whatever subject matter they impart to their students. National standards and benchmarks for both content and teacher preparation in science, mathematics, and technology (AAAS, 1993; NRC, 1996a; NCTM, 2000; ITEA, 2000, AMATYC, 1995) can serve as guides to college-level educators. The CSMTP also recommends that content, pedagogy, and field experiences be planned and implemented jointly with colleagues from schools of education and with school practitioners in a partnership. These joint efforts would lead to better connections between content courses in science, mathematics, and technology; methods courses; and field experiences.

Laboratory and fieldwork, including exercises where students design experiments to answer their own questions, should be an integral component of every science course that prospective teachers take (NRC, 1999h). Learning through inquiry and active engagement with subject matter should be a primary feature of all courses that prospective teachers take—disciplinary as well as pedagogical. Students also should be given as many opportunities as possible to solve problems collaboratively as well as individually.

Educators of teachers, especially those in science, mathematics, engineering departments, must recognize that teachers' content knowledge of science and mathematics grows and matures with time and experience. Thus, teacher education programs, especially for prospective elementary teachers, should offer some coursework in science and mathematics that includes in-depth development of basic ideas of the discipline, reasoning, and problem solving rather than just broad surveys of subject matter. Similarly, programs for experienced teachers should build on those teachers' current content knowledge and help them acquire yet deeper understanding of the subject(s) they teach.

Information technology will permeate and influence virtually every aspect of teaching and learning in the future. Faculty in the content areas and in schools of education together must help teachers learn how to use these tools and how to integrate them into their teaching. Recent reports indicate that teacher education programs are falling far short in providing prospective teachers with such educational opportunities (Becker and Anderson, 1998; Kent and McNergney, 1999; Valdez et al., 1999; Milken Family Foundation, 1999; Means, 2000). Teachers of the future will have to be as cognizant of the capabilities of computers to transform teaching and learning as they are knowledgeable about the primary subject matter they teach (e.g., NRC, 1999a). The national standards and benchmarks for information technology (IT) education released in June 2000 are designed to help teachers use IT to enhance their teaching and their stu-

dents' learning and, therefore, should also help teacher educators better organize their efforts to restructure and improve this critically important component of teacher education.

2. Two- and four-year colleges and universities should reexamine and redesign introductory college-level courses in science and mathematics to better accommodate the needs of practicing and future teachers.

Introductory courses should be structured in ways that help all students better understand the role and relationship of the sciences and mathematics to other disciplines, to students' lives, and to helping students make informed decisions about issues in which science and technology play integral roles.

Most students who do not go on to careers in the sciences do not enroll in courses beyond the introductory level (NSF, 1996; NRC 1999h; AFT, 2000). Moreover, many students either do not know or do not declare their intention to become teachers until later in their college careers (Seymour and Hewitt, 1997). Thus, faculty in the life and physical sciences, mathematics, and engineering who teach lower-division courses in these subjects have a special obligation and responsibility to the education of future teachers. They must understand that any of their students may elect to become teachers and that this decision may not be made until after these students have completed introductory courses. Accordingly, college and university faculty must offer courses that engage all students and provide them with an understanding of the processes as well as the content of their own and related disciplines. These courses also should help all students develop the habits of mind, including curiosity and reflection that prove invaluable for teachers throughout their careers. Specific recommendations about the overarching principles of science that such courses could cover are available (NRC, 1999h).

In short, the development of such introductory and lower division courses should become a higher priority for all science, mathematics, engineering, and technology programs in the nation's two- and four-year colleges and universities. Recommendations about how such courses might be structured have appeared elsewhere (NSF, 1996; McNeal and D'Avanzo, 1997; NRC, 1999h; AMATYC, 1995). The CSMTP agrees fully with those reports that call for SME&T faculty to work much more

closely together to improve the coherence and integration of learning in the SME&T disciplines. Teaching and learning centers could help. For example, in coordination with a campus' teaching and learning center,[2] the pre-teaching advisor or advisory committee could engage SME&T faculty in discussions about adopting new approaches in their disciplinary or interdisciplinary introductory and lower division courses.

3. Universities whose primary mission includes education research should set as a priority the development and execution of peer-reviewed research studies that focus on ways to improve teacher education, the art of teaching, and learning for people of all ages. New research that focuses broadly on synthesizing data across studies and linking it to school practice in a wide variety of school settings would be especially helpful to the improvement of teacher education and professional development for both prospective and experienced teachers. The results of this research

---

[2]Increasing numbers of colleges and universities are establishing teaching and learning centers on their campuses. The University of Kansas maintains a listing of these centers around the world (<http://eagle.cc.ukans.edu/~cte/resources/websites/unitedstates.html>). The goals of the Center for Teaching Excellence at the University of Kansas are to provide opportunities for teaching faculty to discuss students' learning and ways to enhance it in their classrooms; to support faculty as they implement their ideas for improving students' learning; to bring research about teaching to the attention of the university community; to encourage involvement in the scholarship of teaching and research on learning; to offer course development assistance at any stage—planning, teaching, evaluating—to foster instructional innovation; and to advocate and recognize teaching excellence.

should be collated and disseminated through a national electronic database or library.

The National Research Council (1999f) has called for a decade of intensive research on how to improve education. The CSMTP recommends that a major component of this effort be devoted to a comprehensive yet focused examination of how to improve teacher education and teaching in science, mathematics, and technology, as well as how to improve teacher retention in these subject areas.[3] The presidents and chancellors of 61 of the nation's leading research universities already have committed their institutions to engaging in research that will enhance the practice of teaching (e.g., AAU, 1999). The members of the CSMTP applaud this action and urge other institutions of higher education to make similar commitments.

Effective ways must be found to disseminate the results of this research to teachers and to teacher educators. The National Science Foundation is currently investing in the development and construction of a national digital library for SME&T education (NRC, 1998, 1999g; NSF, 2000). The CSMTP recommends that this digital library effort take primary responsibility for collecting, indexing, and broadly disseminating the results of existing and future research on the improvement of teacher education and teaching.

4. Two- and four-year colleges and universities should maintain contact with and provide guidance to teachers who complete their preparation and development programs.[4]

With government agencies, state legislatures, and businesses demanding greater accountability and improvements in the quality of science and

---

[3]The primary sources of federal government support for educational research include numerous programs under the auspices of the Office of the Undersecretary of the U.S. Department of Education (<http://web99.ed.gov/GTEP/Program2.nsf>), the U.S. Department of Education's Office for Educational Research and Improvement (<http://www.ed.gov/offices/OERI/funding.html>), and the National Science Foundation's Division of Research, Evaluation, and Communication (within the Directorate for Education and Human Resources: < http://www.ehr.nsf.gov/ehr/rec/default.htm>). In addition, the American Educational Research Association provides links on its website to its own grants programs and those of other organizations (<http://aera.ucsb.edu/subweb/links-FR.html>).

[4]This recommendation is modeled after a proposal currently under consideration by the Taskforce for K-16 Education of the Association of American Universities (AAU). Under this proposal, a new teacher who graduates from any AAU member institution and relocates to another area served by another AAU member institution would be invited to participate in a variety of professional and social activities with other teachers in the area. Such reciprocal agreements would enable teachers who have relocated to interact with other teachers with similar backgrounds and allow universities to maintain better records about the professional activities of their graduates. The CSMTP strongly supports this kind of networking and urges other higher education organizations to undertake similar ventures with their member institutions.

mathematics teaching in the United States, it is in the interests of colleges and universities to know how their teacher graduates are faring. Colleges and universities that prepare teachers should (1) keep track of their graduates' careers in teaching and (2) determine their graduates' job performance and other measures of teaching success through questionnaires to the teachers themselves and to leaders at the schools where they are employed. Keeping track of these students would allow institutions of higher education to undertake research both on the career paths of teachers and on the academic performance of the teachers' students. This information also could be used to target improvements in teacher education programs.

New teachers also could benefit greatly by maintaining formal official and informal contacts with their alma mater's education programs. The social, cultural, and intellectual environments of college and university campuses offer important opportunities for new teachers to grow professionally. Thus, the CSMTP agrees with the American Council on Education (1999) in recommending that all institutions of higher education that educate teachers find ways to include their graduates in the life and activities of their campuses for at least three years following graduation. This contact might include invita-

tions to new teachers to join listservs or chat rooms so that they may discuss common issues and concerns about teaching. Other ways to maintain such contact would be to invite teacher alumni/ae back to the campus in summer to participate in graduate-level or informal courses on topics of particular relevance to novice teachers. These courses and programs might include more in-depth study of content matter in science and mathematics; opportunities to undertake research projects with faculty, graduate students, or fellow teachers from local partnerships; and symposia and other presentations that deal with science, mathematics, and education.

Given the near ubiquity of access to the Internet, teachers who are in remote locations could still participate in electronic discussion groups and Webcasts of lectures and symposia sponsored by their undergraduate or graduate institutions.

5. Following a period of collaborative planning and preparation, two- and four-year colleges and universities in a partnership for teacher education should assume primary responsibility for providing professional development opportunities to experienced teachers of science, mathematics, and technology. Such programs would involve faculty from science, mathematics, and engineer-

ing disciplines and from schools of education.

As described elsewhere in this report, two-year community colleges are playing increasingly critical roles in educating students who are likely to pursue careers in teaching. Hence, full participation will be required of two-year colleges in both formal partnerships and in other kinds of arrangements to promote improved teacher education. Additional recommendations concerning these kinds of collaborative activities are detailed below (see RECOMMENDATIONS FOR THE K-12 Community, Recommendation #3).

RECOMMENDATIONS FOR THE K-12 COMMUNITY

1. Following a period of collaborative planning and preparation, school districts in a partnership for teacher education should assume primary responsibility for providing high-quality practicum experiences and internships for prospective teachers.

Currently, local school districts serve as laboratories that provide prospective teachers with opportunities to obtain classroom experience. However, most of the funds to support these practicum programs come from the two- and four-year colleges and universities that prepare future teachers.

The CSMTP proposes that this arrangement change and that, in concert with local teacher education partnerships, school districts take primary responsibility for developing and implementing practicum experiences for preservice teachers, piloting various ways to handle this responsibility over time to test for the most effective arrangements. This proposal would be of benefit to both districts and prospective teachers because districts have a much better appreciation of their staffing needs and how student teachers and teacher internships might address them than do the colleges and universities that supply those student teachers. The activities to come under the direct sponsorship and supervision of districts would include early field experiences for students who are just beginning their teacher education programs, field placement with a master or mentor teacher for more prolonged student teaching experience, and induction-level internships for recent graduates with baccalaureate degrees. In addition, the master or mentor teachers and school district administrators could work through a partnership arrangement with the pre-teaching advisors from the collaborating college or university (see also Recommendations for Collaboration Between Institutions of Higher Education and the K-12 Community.

To support this new arrangement, the CSMTP recommends that funds previously allocated by the institutions of higher education for this purpose be redirected instead to the supervising school districts. This loss of funds by departments or colleges of education would be offset by their assumption of primary responsibility for professional development for teachers in the partner districts (see also Chapter 6, Financial Support for Partnerships for Teacher Education).

2. School districts in a partnership for teacher education should assume primary responsibility for developing and overseeing field experiences, student teaching, and internship programs for new teachers of science, mathematics, and technology.

In cooperation with their partnership for teacher education, school districts should create infrastructures that allow new teachers sufficient time for professional development. Up to 20 percent of a beginning teacher's workweek should be set aside for planning, discussions with mentor teachers, and for additional coursework in the subjects he or she is teaching in the first year of employment. This kind of plan would require flexible, creative, and individualized scheduling that meets the needs of the novice teacher. Teachers who are given this opportunity would agree after their

internship to work with and assist mentors to other new teachers who enter the school or district in subsequent years.

If teaching is to be viewed as comparable with other respected professions in our society, then schools, districts, and states must recognize that beginning teachers do not possess all of the content knowledge and pedagogical skills they need to be maximally effective. Novice teachers must be afforded the time and opportunities for meaningful professional development. A number of districts and states have recognized this critical need and have begun to implement systemically opportunities for all beginning teachers to take workday time for reflection and activities outside the classroom that contribute to their effectiveness in the classroom. Descriptions of such programs are provided in Appendix D.

The CSMTP applauds these kinds of programs and urges all school districts and states to adopt similar strategies. Funds to support such efforts could come from a variety of sources. For example, some portion of the funds districts use to provide professional development programs for all teachers could be reallocated to the internship program. Professional development funds available to schools and districts from national programs could be tapped. States also could be a source.

How is professional expertise in teaching developed? Expert teachers that I have known do not acquire expertise simply by listening to lectures about content, about learning, or about pedagogy. Although I have seen gifted beginning teachers, [this] sort of expertise . . . typically requires guided practical experience and on-going professional development throughout a career. In addition to having resources and opportunities available to them, it requires significant desire and time investment on the part of the developing teacher. The development of what expertise I have as a teacher has paralleled my development as a learner. I have experienced and observed the world of the classroom, enjoyed the guidance of a mentor, interacted within a community of colleagues, and taken on my own investigations in the nature of teaching and learning. The benefits I enjoyed as a developing learner about teaching are similar to those that I attempt to create in the environment for learning for my precollege students.

Minstrell, 1999, page 9

The CSMTP specifically recommends that states explore emulating California's contributions to internship programs for new teachers (Halford, 1998). *However, the CSMTP reiterates that the primary source of funds for such activities should come from multi-year, line items in the budgets of partnerships to which all of the partners contribute.*

3. School districts should collaborate with two- and four-year colleges and universities to provide professional development opportunities to experienced teachers of science, mathematics, and technology. Such programs would involve faculty from science, mathematics, and engineering disciplines and from schools of education. Teachers who participate in these programs would, in turn, offer their expertise and guidance to others involved with the partnership.

The CSMTP calls on school districts to work closely with local colleges and universities in their partnership to develop graduate-level programs for teachers of science, mathematics, and technology. Discussions among teachers engaged in such a program predictably would be high level and in-depth. Such collaboration also would promote the establishment of learning communities and a culture of lifelong learning for teachers as they progress through their careers (e.g., Resnick and Hall, 1998; Fullan, 1993). By design, these programs should allow practicing teachers to enhance their understanding and appreciation of the subject(s) they teach. They should be structured in accordance with guidelines that other organizations have published about what teachers of science and mathematics should know and be able to do to teach effectively at various grade levels. Such programs also should encourage teachers to learn about and discuss modern educational theory, theories of learning, and related subjects.

Both two- and four-year colleges and universities could be involved with these professional development programs. Through the kinds of partnerships discussed in Chapter 6, two-and four-year colleges and universities could decide how best to apportion responsibility for conducting these programs. For example, with appropriate support from universities in the partnership, community colleges might offer courses with graduate credit to experienced teachers.

It should be noted here that the model for ongoing teacher professional development articulated in Figure 6-4

also calls for professional development of teachers that would allow them to become mentors to other teachers and to faculty counterparts and students in higher education, as well as leaders in their districts. One avenue for leadership for mentor teachers would be to become closely involved with their district/college partnership. Teachers who progressed through partnership programs might reasonably be expected to serve as participants or leaders in policymaking arenas in their districts, such as curriculum, as well as to serve as mentors to other teachers. Master or mentor teachers also could serve as liaisons to local college and university partners or in other ways that benefited the partnership's community. For example, they could provide invaluable perspective and expertise to the improvement of design and execution of professional development programs in the partnership. They also could work directly with teacher educators and students to strengthen preservice and other activities. Working to enhance the teaching profession is something teachers not only should be encouraged and supported to do but something for which they should take responsibility, as do other professionals for their professions. In this way, teaching could take on more of the supportive infrastructure and stature that other professions enjoy.

These types of expectations of teachers must be coupled, however, with the district's willingness to provide experienced teachers with time during their work hours and throughout the school year. The kinds of partnership or collaborations envisioned by the CSMTP here could ease the district's burden in this regard. For example, qualified student teachers who have been mentored closely through the partnership might be able to provide the needed classroom coverage.

The CSMTP recognizes that implementation of this recommendation might be difficult for school districts not located near colleges or universities. However, the use of distance learning and other types of information technologies would allow teachers from locations that are geographically removed from the partnership to participate in these kinds of courses (e.g., Ariza et al., 2000).

RECOMMENDATIONS FOR PROFESSIONAL AND DISCIPLINARY ORGANIZATIONS

1. Organizations that represent institutions of higher education should assist their members in establishing programs to help new teachers. For example, databases of information about new teachers would be developed and shared among member institutions so that colleges and universities could be notified when a newly certified teacher was moving to their area to teach. Those colleges and universities could then plan and offer welcoming and support activities, such as opportunities for continued professional and intellectual growth. Models for this kind of support for new teachers are described elsewhere in this report.

2. Professional disciplinary societies in science, mathematics, and engineering, higher education organizations, government at all levels, and business and industry should become more engaged partners (as opposed to advisors or overseers) in efforts to improve teacher education.

3. Professional disciplinary societies in science, mathematics, and engineering, and higher education organizations also should work together to align their policies and recommendations for improving teacher education in science, mathematics, and engineering. In addition to the societies that serve the professional needs of teachers, many disciplinary research organizations have become more interested in improving science and mathematics education in grades K-12. A number of these organizations are beginning to focus on how they can become more involved with improving teacher education. Profes-

Statement on the Education of Future Teachers

The scientific societies listed below urge the physics community, specifically physical science and engineering departments and their faculty members, to take an active role in improving the preservice training of K-12 physics/science teachers. Improving teacher training involves building cooperative working relationships between physicists in universities and colleges and the individuals and groups involved in teaching physics to K-12 students. Strengthening the science education of future teachers addresses the pressing national need for improving K-12 physics education and recognizes that these teachers play a critical education role as the first and often-time last physics teacher for most students.

While this responsibility can be manifested in many ways, research indicates that effective preservice education involves hands-on, laboratory-based learning. Good science and mathematics education will help create a scientifically literate public, capable of making informed decisions on public policy involving scientific matters. A strong K-12 physics education is also the first step in producing the next generation of researchers, innovators, and technical workers.

American Institute of Physics
American Physical Society
American Association of Physics Teachers
American Astronomical Society
Acoustical Society of America

American Institute of Physics, December 1999[5]

---

[5]This statement and a cover letter to chairs of departments of physics and astronomy are available at <http://www.aip.org/education/futeach.htm>.

sional societies in science, mathematics, and engineering have the potential to play a critical role in improving teacher education. However, the various disciplines must find ways to work together to develop and implement teacher education programs and activities that are in concert with recommendations from national organizations and that promote consistent goals for each discipline. The CSMTP calls on umbrella organizations such as the Council of Scientific Society Presidents or others in specific disciplines to begin this dialogue by convening representatives from professional societies to discuss their individual and collective roles in teacher education.

References

Abdal-Haqq, Ismat. 1998. *Professional Development Schools: Weighing the Evidence.* Thousand Oaks, CA: Corwin Press.

Accreditation Board for Engineering and Technology (ABET). 1997. *Engineering Criteria 2000, 3rd ed.* Baltimore, MD: Author.

American Association for the Advancement of Science (AAAS). 1989. *Science for All Americans.* Washington, DC: Author.

AAAS. 1990. *The Liberal Art of Science: Agenda for Action.* Washington, DC: Author.

AAAS. 1993. *Benchmarks for Science Literacy.* New York: Oxford University Press.

American Association of Community Colleges (AACC). 2000. *National Community College Snapshot.* Washington, DC: Author. Available at <http://199.75.76.25/allaboutcc/snapshot.htm>

American Chemical Society (ACS). 1989. *Recommendations for the Education of Chemistry Teachers.* Washington, DC: American Chemical Society Committee on Education.

American Council on Education (ACE). 1999. *To Touch the Future: Transforming the Way Teachers Are Taught. An Action Agenda for College and University Presidents.* Washington, DC: Author.

American Federation of Teachers (AFT). 2000. *Building a Profession: Strengthening Teacher Preparation and Induction.* Report of the K-16 Teacher Education Task Force. Washington, DC: Author. Also available at <http://www.aft.org/higher_ed/reports/K16report.html>.

American Institute of Physics (AIP). 1999. Statement on the Education of Future Teachers. College Park, MD: Author. Available at <http://www.aip.org/education/futeach.htm>.

American Mathematical Association of Two-Year Colleges (AMATYC). 1995. *Crossroads in Mathematics: Standards for Introductory College Mathematics Before Calculus.* Memphis, TN.: Author.

Anderson, R.D., and Mitchener, C.P. 1994. *Research on Science Teacher Education. Handbook of Research on Science Teaching and Learning.* National Science Teachers Association. New York: Macmillan Publishing.

Apple. M. (ed.). 1997. *Review of Research in Education.* Washington, DC: American Educational Research Association.

Ariza, E.N., Knee, R.H., and Ridge, M.L. 2000. "Uniting teachers to embrace 21st century technology: A critical mass in a cohort of colleagues." *Technological Horizons in Education.* 27(10): 22-30.

Arons, A.B. 1990. *A Guide to Introductory Physics Teaching.* New York: John Wiley and Sons.

Asimov, N. 1999. "Neediest students get least-prepared teachers." *San Francisco Chronicle,* Dec. 3, 1999. Also available at <http://www.sfgate.com/cgi-bin/article.cgi?file=/chronicle/archive/1999/12/03/MN45594.DTL>.

Association for the Education of Teachers of Science (AETS). 1997. *Professional Standards for Science Teacher Educators.* Available at <http://www.aets.unr.edu>.

Association of American Universities (AAU). 1999. "Resolution on Teacher Education." Washington, DC: Association of American

Universities. Available at <http://www.tulane.edu/~aau/TeacherEdRes.html>.

Bacon, W.S. 2000. *Bringing the Excitement of Science to the Classroom: Using Summer Research Programs to Invigorate High School Science.* Tucson, AZ: Research Corporation.

Ball, D.L. 1988. "Research on teacher learning: Studying how teachers' knowledge changes." *Action in Teacher Education* 10(2): 17-24.

Ball, D.L. 1990. "Prospective elementary and secondary teachers' understanding of division. *"Journal for Research in Mathematics Education* 21: 132-144.

Ball, D.L. 1997. "Developing Mathematics Reform: What Don't We Know About Teacher Learning-But Would Make Good Working Hypotheses." In Friel, S.N., and Bright, G.W. (eds.), *Reflecting on Our Work: NSF Teacher Enhancement in Mathematics.* New York: University Press of America.

Ball, D.L. 1998. "Unlearning to teach mathematics." *For the Learning of Mathematics* 8(1): 40-48.

Ball, D.L., and Wilson, S.M. 1990. "Becoming a Mathematics Teacher through College-Based and Alternate Routes: The Relationship between Knowing Your Subject and Learning to Teach It." Paper presented at the annual meeting of the American Educational Research Association, April 1990, Boston.

Becker, H.J. 1990. "Computer use in the United States: 1989. An initial report of U.S. participation in the IEA computers in education survey." Paper presented at the annual meeting of the American Educational Research Association, April 1990, Boston.

Becker, H.J., and Anderson, R. 1998. "Teaching, Learning, and Computing: 1998." Available at <http://www.crito.uci.edu/tlc/html/findings.html>.

Biehle, J.T., Motz, L.L, and West, S.S. 1999. *NSTA Guide to School Science Facilities.* Arlington, VA: National Science Teachers Association.

Boles, K., and Troen, V. 1997. "How the emergence of teacher leadership helped build a professional development school." In Levine, M. and Trachtman, R. (eds.), *Making Professional Development Schools Work.* New York: Teachers College Press.

Borko, H., et al. 1993. "To teach mathematics for conceptual or procedural knowledge? A dilemma of learning to teach in the New World

Order of mathematics education reform." *Journal for Research in Mathematics Education* 24(2): 2-23.

Boyer, S., and Layman, J.1998. "CEPT Guidelines: introduction." In NSF Collaboratives for Excellence in Teacher Preparation: Guidelines for Reform. Fourth annual CEPT meeting in Arlington, Virginia. Washington DC: National Science Foundation.

Brandt, R., ed. 2000. *Education in a New Era.* Alexandria, VA: Association for Supervision and Curriculum Development.

Brennan, S., Thames, W., and Roberts, R. 1999. "Kentucky—Mentoring for Success." *Educational Leadership* 56(8): 49-52.

Brown, C.A., and Borko, H. 1992. *Becoming a Mathematics Teacher.* In Grouws, D.A. (ed.), *Handbook of Research on Mathematics Teaching and Learning.* New York: Macmillan Publishing.

Brown, C.A., Silver, E.A., and Smith, M.S. 1995. *The Missing Link in Mathematics Instructional Reform in Urban Schools: The Assistance Provided by Resource Partners in the QUASAR Project.* Presentation at the annual meeting of the American Educational Research Association, San Francisco, April.

Byrd, D.M., and McIntyre, S.J. 1999. *Research on Professional Development Schools: Teacher Education Yearbook VII.* Thousand Oaks, CA: Corwin Press,

Callan, P.M., and Usdan, M.D. 1999. "Two different worlds." *American School Board Journal,* December issue. pp. 44-46.

Carlsen, W.S. 1987. "Why do you ask? The effects of science teacher subject-matter knowledge on teacher questioning and classroom discourse." Paper presented at the annual meeting of the American Educational Research Association (ERIC Document Reproduction Service NO.ED 293: 181).

Carlsen, W. 1988. "The effect of science teacher subject matter knowledge on teacher questioning and classroom discourse. Unpublished doctoral dissertation." Stanford University, CA.

Carpenter, T.P., Fennema, E., Petersen, P. L., and Carey, D. 1988. "Teachers' pedagogical content knowledge of students' problem solving in elementary arithmetic." *Journal for Research in Mathematics Education* 19: 385-401.

Carpenter, T.P., Fennema, A., Peterson, P.L., Chiang, C., and Loef, M. 1989. "Using knowledge of children's mathematics thinking in classroom teaching: an experimental study." *Educational Research Journal* 26(4): 499-531.

CEO Forum on Education and Technology. 1999. "Professional Development: A Link to Better Learning." The CEO Forum School Technology and Readiness Report. Washington, DC: Author.

CEO Forum on Education and Technology. 2000. "Repairing a New Generation of Teachers—Teacher Preparation STaR Chart: A Self-Assessment Tool for Colleges of Education." Washington, DC: Author.

Chaney, B 1995. "Student outcomes and the professional preparation of eighth-grade teachers in science and mathematics: NSF/NELS." Rockville, MD: Westat.

Coble, C.R., and Koballa, T. R. 1996. *Science Education. Handbook of Research on Science Teaching and Learning.* National Science Teachers Association. New York: Macmillan Publishing.

Cochran, K.F. 1997. "Pedagogical content knowledge: Teachers' integration of subject matter, pedagogy, students, and learning environments." Brief. *Research Matters – to the Science Teacher.* No. 9702. National Association of Research in Science Teaching.

Cohen, D.K., and Hill, H.C. 1998. *Instructional Policy and Classroom Performance: The Mathematics Reform in California.* CPRE Research Report Series. RR-39.

Coleman, J.S., Campbell, E.Q., Hobson, C.J., McPortland, J., Mood, A.M., Weinfield, E.D., and York, R. 1966. "Equality of Educational Opportunity." Washington DC: U.S. Government Printing Office.

Conference Board of the Mathematical Sciences (CBMS). In preparation. "CBMS Mathematical Education of Teachers Project." Draft Report, - March 2000. Available at <http://www.maa.org/cbms/metdraft/index.htm>

Confrey, J., Castro-Filho, J., and Wilhelm, J. In press. "Implementation research as a means to link systemic reform and applied psychology in mathematics education." *Educational Psychologist.*

Cooney, T.J. 1994. "Teacher education as an exercise in adaptation." In: Aichele, D.B. and Coxford, A.F. (eds.), *Professional Development for Teachers of Mathematics, 1994 Yearbook* Reston, VA: National Council of Teachers of Mathematics. pp. 9-22.

Cuban, L., and Kirkpatrick, H. 1998. "Computers make kids smarter, right?" *Technos* 7(2): 26-31.

Darling-Hammond, L. 1997. *The Right to Learn: A Blueprint for Creating Schools that Work.* San Francisco: Jossey-Bass.

Darling-Hammond, L. 1998. "Teachers and Teaching: Testing Policy Hypotheses from a National Commission Report." *Educational Researcher* 27(1): 5-15.

Darling-Hammond, L., and Berry, B. 1998. "Investing in Teaching: The Dividend Is Student Achievement." *Education Week*, May 27, 1998, p. 48.

Darling-Hammond, L., and Macdonald, M.B. 2000. "Where There Is Learning There Is Hope: The Preparation of Teachers at the Bank Street College of Education." In Darling-Hammond, L. (ed.). *Studies of Excellence in Teacher Education: Preparation at the Graduate Level.* Washington, DC: American Association of Colleges for Teacher Education. pp. 1-95.

Del Prete, T. 1997. "The rounds model of professional development." *From the Inside* 1(1): 12-13.

Dietz, M.E. 1999. "Critical Components in the Preparation of Teachers." In Roth, R.A. (ed.) *The Role of the University in the Preparation of Teachers.* Philadelphia, PA: Falmer Press, pp. 226-240.

Downes, S. 2000. "Commentary: Nine Rules for Good Technology." *Technology Source*, July/August issue. Also available at <http://horizon.unc.edu/TS/commentary/2000-07a.asp>.

Druva, C.A., and Anderson, R.D. 1983. "Science Teacher Characteristics by Teacher Behavior and by Student Outcome: A Meta-Analysis of Research."*Journal of Research in Science Training* 20(5): 467-479.

Edelfelt, R. (ed.). 1999. "University-School Teacher Education Partnerships: First Year Report." Chapel Hill, NC: University of North Carolina. Also available at <http://www.ga.unc.edu/21stcenturyschools/reports/>.

Education Commission of the States. 2000. *In Pursuit of Quality Teaching: Five Key Strategies for Policymakers.* Denver, CO: Author.

Education Trust. 1998. "Good Teaching Matters—How Well-Qualified Teachers Can Close the Gap." *Thinking K-16* 3(2).

Education Week. 2000. "Quality Counts 2000: Who Should Teach?" Available at <http://www.edweek.org/sreports/qc00/>.

Feistritzer, C.E. 1999a. "The Evolution of Alternative Teacher Certification." *The Educational Forum* 58, Winter Edition, 132-138.

Feistritzer, C.E. 1999b. *The Making of a Teacher: A Report on Teacher Preparation in the U.S.* Washington, DC: Center for Education Information.

Feistritzer, C.E., and Chester, D.T. 2000. *Alternative Teacher Certification: a State-by-State Analysis.* Washington DC: National Center for Education Information.

Fennema, E., and Franke, M.L. 1992. "Teachers' knowledge and its impact." In: Grouws, D.A. (ed.), *Handbook of Research on Mathematics Teaching and Learning.* Reston, VA: National Council of Teachers of Mathematics.

Ferguson, R.F. 1991. "Paying for public education: new evidence on how and why money matters." *Harvard Journal on Legislation* 28(2): 465-498.

Ferguson, R.F., and Ladd, H.F. 1996. "How and Why Money Matters: An Analysis of Alabama Schools. "In Ladd, Helen (ed.), *Holding Schools Accountable.* Washington DC: The Brookings Institution.

Fetler, M. 1999. "High School Staff Characteristics and Mathematics Test Results." *Education Policy Analysis Archives* 7(9): 1-19.

Fideler, E.F., and Haselkorn, D. 1999. *Learning the Ropes: Urban Teacher Induction Programs and Practices in the United States.* Belmont, MA: Recruiting New Teachers.

Flexner, A. 1910. "Medical education in the United States and Canada: a report to the Carnegie Foundation for the Advancement of Teaching." *New York: Bulletin of the Carnegie Foundation for the Advancement of Teaching, Vol. 4.*

Fuhrman, H., and Massell, D. 1992. *Issues and Strategies in Systemic Reform.* New Brunswick, NJ and Philadelphia, PA: Consortium for Policy Research in Education (CPRE).

Fullan, M.G. 1993. Why Teachers Must Become Change Agents. *Educational Leadership* 50(6).

Gess-Newsome, J., and Lederman, N. 1993. "Preservice biology teachers' knowledge structures as a function of professional teacher education: A year-long assessment." *Science Education* 77, 25-45.

Good, T., Biddle, B., and Brophy, J. 1975. *Teachers Make a Difference.* New York: Holt, Rinehart and Winston.

Goodlad, J. 1990. *Teachers for Our Nation's Schools.* San Francisco: Jossey-Bass.

Goodlad, J. 1994. *Educational Renewal: Better Teachers, Better Schools.* San Francisco: Jossey-Bass.

Grouws, D.A., and Schultz, K.A. 1996. In Sikula, J. (ed.), *Handbook of Research on Teacher Education, 2nd ed.* New York: Macmillan.

Halford, J.M. 1998. "Easing the way for new teachers." *Educational Leadership* 55(5): 33-36.

Hanushek, E.A. 1992. "The Trade-off between Child Quantity and Quality." *Journal of Political Economy* 100(1): 84-117.

Harmon, M., Smith, T.A., Martin, M.O., Kelly, D.L., Beaton, A.E, Mullis, I.V.S., Gonzalez, E.J., and Orpwood, G. 1997. *Performance Assessment in IEA's Third International Mathematics and Science Study.* Chestnut Hill, MA: International Association for the Evaluation of Educational Achievement.

Hart, P.D. Research Associates, Inc. 1999. "Key Findings from Research on Young Americans' Interest in the Public School Teaching Profession." Report commissioned by the Milken Family Foundation. Santa Monica, CA: Milken Family Foundation.

Haselkorn, D., and Harris, L. 1998. *The Essential Profession: a National Survey of Public Attitudes Toward Teaching, Educational Opportunity, and School Reform.* Belmont, MA: Recruiting New Teachers.

Hashweh, M.Z. 1986. "An exploratory study of teacher knowledge and teaching: the effects of science teachers' knowledge of subject matter and their conceptions of learning on their teaching." Doctoral dissertation, Stanford University, 1985. *Dissertation Abstracts International* 46:3672A.

Hashweh, M. 1987. "Effects of subject matter knowledge in the teaching of biology and physics." *Teaching and Teacher Education* 3(2): 109-120.

Hawk, P., Coble, C., and Swanson, M. 1985. "Certification: It Does Matter." *Journal of Teacher Education.* May-June issue.

Hawkins, E.F., Stancavage, F.B., and Dossey, J.A. 1998. "School Policies and Practices Affecting Instruction in Mathematics: Findings from the National Assessment of Educational Progress." National Center for Education Statistics. Office of Educational Research and Improvement.

Washington, DC: U.S. Government Printing Office.

Henderson, D. 2000. "Texas Teachers, Moonlighting, and Morale: 1980-2000." Austin, TX: Texas State Teachers Association.

Heuser, D., and Owens, R.F. 1999. "Planting Seeds, Planting Teachers." *Educational Leadership* 56(8): 53-56.

Hirsch, E. 2000. "Teacher Pay for Performance." *LegisBrief Series*. Washington, DC: National Council of State Legislatures.

Hoff, D.L. 2000. "Science Teachers' Turnover Dissatisfaction High, Survey Finds." *Education Week*. April 19, 2000.

Holmes Group. 1986. *Tomorrow's Teachers*. East Lansing, MI: The Holmes Group. Summary available at <http://www.baylor.edu/~SOE/SCHOLMES/TT.HTML>.

Holmes Group. 1990. *Tomorrow's Schools: Principles for the Design of Professional Development Schools*. East Lansing, MI: The Holmes Group.

Holmes Group. 1995. *Tomorrow's Schools of Education*. East Lansing, MI: The Holmes Group.

Houston, W.R., Hollis, L.Y., Clay, D., Ligons, C.M., and Roff, L. 1999. "The Effects of Collaboration on Urban Teacher Education Programs and Professional Development Schools." In *Research on Professional Development Schools, Teacher Education Yearbook VII*. Thousand Oaks, CA: Corwin Press.

Howard Hughes Medical Institute. 1996. *Beyond BIO 101*. Chevy Chase, MD: Author.

Howey, K. 1996. "Designing Coherent and Effective Teacher Education Programs." In: Sikula, J., Buttery, T., and Guyton, E. (eds.). *Handbook of Research on Teacher Education, 2nd ed.* New York: Macmillan. pp. 143-170.

Huling-Austin, L., 1992. "Research on Learning to Teach: Implications for Teacher Induction and Mentoring Programs." *Journal of Teacher Education* 43(3): 173-180.

Imel, S. 1992. "Reflective Practice in Adult Education." ERIC Digest No. 122. Also available at <http://www.ed.gov/databases/ERIC_Digests/ed346319.html>.

Ingersoll, R.M. 1999. "The Problem of Underqualified Teachers in American Secondary Schools." *Educational Researcher* 28(2): 26-37.

International Technology Education Association (ITEA). 2000. *Standards for Technological Literacy: Content for the Study of Technology*. Reston, VA: Author.

Interstate New Teacher Support Consortium (INTASC). 1999. *Core Standards*. See <http://facstaff.uww.edu/speced/course/INTASC_Standards.htm >. See also <http://www.ccsso.org/intascst.html>.

Kelley, C., Odden, A., Milanowski, A., and Heneman III, H. 2000. "The Motivational Effects of School-Based Performance Awards." *CPRE Policy Briefs*. February ed. Philadelphia, PA: University of Pennsylvania Graduate School of Education.

Kent, T., and McNergney, R. 1999. *Will Technology Really Change Education? From Blackboard to Web*. Thousand Oaks, CA: Corwin Press.

King, B., and Newman, F.M. 2000. "Will Teacher Learning Advance School Goals?" *Phi Delta Kappan* 81(8): 576.

Knuth, R., Hopey, C., and Rocap, K. (eds.) 1996. *Guiding Questions for Technology Planning*. Oak Brook, IL: North Central Regional Educational Laboratory. Available at <http://www.ncrtec.org/capacity/guidewww/gqhome.htm>.

Koppich, J.K. 2000. "Trinity University: Preparing Teachers for Tomorrow's Schools." In Darling-Hammond, L. (ed.). *Studies of Excellence in Teacher Education: Preparation in a Five- Year Program*. Washington, DC: American Association of Colleges for Teacher Education. pp. 1-48.

Lampert, M., and Ball, D.L. 1990. "Using hypermedia technology to support a new pedagogy of teacher education." Issue paper No. 90-5. Lansing, MI: National Center for Research on Teacher Education.

Lampert, M., and Ball, D.L. 1998. *Teaching, Multimedia, and Mathematics: Investigations of Real Practice*. New York: Teachers College Press.

Learning First Alliance. 1998. *Every Child Mathematically Proficient: An Action Plan*. Washington, DC: Author.

Lederman, N.G., and Gess-Newsome, J. 1999. *Examining Pedagogical Content Knowledge*. The Netherlands: Kluwer Academic Publishers.

Lewis, J., and Tucker, A. In press. *The Mathematics Education of Teachers*. See <www.maa.org/cbms>.

Lewis, L., Snow, K., Farris, E. Smerdon, B., Cronen, S., Kaplan, J., and Greene, B. 2000. *Condition of America's Public School Facilities:*

1999. NCES 2000-032. National Center for Education Statistics. Washington, DC: U.S. Department of Education. Also available at <http://nces.ed.gov/pubsearch/pubsinfo.asp?pubid=2000032>.

Loucks-Horsley, S., Bybee, R.W., and Wild, E.L.C. 1996. "The Role of Community Colleges in the Professional Development of Science Teachers." *Journal of College Science Teaching* 26(2): 130-134.

Loucks-Horsley, S., Hewson, P.W., Love, N., and Stiles, K.E. 1998. *Designing Professional Development for Teachers of Science and Mathematics.* Thousand Oaks, CA: Corwin Press.

Loucks-Horsley, S., and Matsumoto, C. 1999. "Research on professional development for teachers of mathematics and science: the state of the scene." *School Science and Mathematics* 99(5): 258-271.

Loughran, J. 1997. "Teaching about teaching: principles and practice." In Loughran, J., and Russell, T., *Teaching about Teaching: Purpose, Passion, and Pedagogy in Teacher Education.* Washington, DC: Falmer Press.

Ma, L. 1999. *Knowing and Teaching Elementary Mathematics: Teachers' Understanding of Fundamental Mathematics in China and the United States.* Mahwah, NJ: Lawrence Erlbaum Associates.

Mangan, K.S. 2000. "Aviation centers take off as airlines face pilot shortfall." *Chronicle of Higher Education* 46(20), A47

McCullough, L., and Mintz, S. 1992. "Concerns of preservice students in the USA about the practice of teaching." *Journal of Education for Teaching* 18(1): 59-67.

McDiarmid, G.W., Ball, D.L., and Anderson, C.W. 1989. "Why staying ahead one chapter doesn't really work: Subject-specific pedagogy." In Reynolds, M.C. (ed.), *Knowledge Base for the Beginning Teacher.* New York: Pergamon.

McIntyre, J., Byrd, D. and Foxx, S. 1996. Field and Laboratory Experiences. In *Handbook of Research on Teacher Education, 171-193,* 2nd ed. Sikula, J. (ed.), New York: Macmillan Library.

McNeal, A.P., and D'Avanzo, C.D. (eds.). 1997. *Student Active Science: Models of Innovation in College Science Teaching.* Fort Worth, TX: Harcourt Brace.

Manouchehri, A. 1997. "School Mathematics Reform: Implications for Mathematics Teacher Preparation." *Journal of Teacher Education* 48 (3).

Maryland State Department of Education. 1998. "Recommendations of Strategic Directions for Professional Development in Maryland's Public Schools, 1996-2000." Fact Sheet 42. Annapolis, MD: Author. See also <http://www.msde.state.md.us/fact%20sheets/fact42.html>.

Mathematical Association of America (MAA). 1991. *A Call for Change: Recommendations for the Mathematical Preparation of Teachers of Mathematics.* Leitzel, J.R.C. (ed.). Washington, DC: Author.

Means, B. 2000. "Technology in America's Schools: Before and After Y2K." In Brandt, Ron (ed.), *Education in a New Era.* Alexandria, VA: Association for Supervision and Curriculum Development.

Merseth, K.K., 1993. How old is the shepherd? An essay about mathematics education. *Phi Delta Kappan* 74: 548-554.

Merseth, K.K., and Koppich, J.K. 2000. "Teacher Education at the University of Virginia: A Study of English and Mathematics Preparation." In Darling-Hammond, L. (ed.), *Studies of Excellence in Teacher Education: Preparation in a Five-Year Program.* Washington, DC: American Association of Colleges for Teacher Education. pp. 49-81.

Milken Family Foundation. 1999. "Will New Teachers Be Prepared to Teach in a Digital Age?: A National Survey on Information Technology in Teacher Education." Los Angeles, CA: Milken Family Foundation. Available at <http://www.mff.org/publications/>.

Minstrell, J. 1999. "Expertise in Teaching." In Sternberg, R. and Horvath, J. (eds.), *Tacit Knowledge in Professional Practice.* Mahwah, NJ: Erlbaum.

Mundry, S., Spector, B., Stiles, K., and Loucks-Horsley, S. 1999. *Working Toward a Continuum of Professional Learning Experiences for Teachers of Science and Mathematics.* Madison, WI: National Center for Science Education, University of Wisconsin.

Murnane, R.J., and Levy, F. 1997. "The new basics." *American School Board Journal.* April issue, pp. 26-29.

Murray, F.B. 1996. "Beyond Natural Teaching:

The Case for Professional Education." In *The Teacher Educator's Handbook: Building a Knowledge Base for the Preparation of Teachers*. San Francisco: Jossey-Bass.

National Association of Biology Teachers (NABT). 1990. "Characteristics of an Outstanding Biology Teacher." Position statement of the Board of Directors. Reston, VA: Author. Available at <http://www.nabt.org/characteristics.html>.

National Board for Professional Teaching Standards (NBPTS). 1994. *What Teachers Should Know and Be Able to Do.* Detroit, MI: Author.

National Commission on Excellence in Education (NCEE). 1983. *A Nation at Risk: The Imperative for Educational Reform.* Washington, DC: U.S. Department of Education. Also available at <http://www.ed.gov/pubs/NatAtRisk/>.

National Commission on Mathematics and Science Teaching for the 21st Century. 2000. *Before It's Too Late.* Jessup, MD: Education Publications Center.

National Commission on Teaching and America's Future (NCTAF). 1996. *What Matters Most: Teaching for America's Future.* New York: Author.

NCTAF. 1997. *Doing What Matters Most: Investing in Quality Teaching.* New York: Author.

National Council for Accreditation of Teacher Education (NCATE). 2000. *NCATE 2000 Unit Standards.* Washington, DC: Author. Available at < http://www.ncate.org/2000/pressrelease.htm>

National Council of Teachers of Mathematics (NCTM). 1989. *Curriculum and Evaluation Standards for School Mathematics.* Reston, VA: Author.

NCTM. 1991. *Professional Standards for Teaching Mathematics.* Reston, VA: Author.

NCTM. 2000. *Principles and Standards for School Mathematics.* Reston, VA: Author.

National Research Council (NRC). 1989. *Everybody Counts: A Report to the Nation on the Future of Mathematics Education.* Washington, DC: National Academy Press. Also available at <http://books.nap.edu/books/0309039770/html/97.html>.

NRC. 1990. *Reshaping School Mathematics: A Philosophy and Framework for Curriculum.* Washington, DC: National Academy Press. Also available at <http://books.nap.edu/catalog/1498.html>.

NRC. 1991. *Moving Beyond Myths: Revitalizing Undergraduate Mathematics.* Washington, DC: National Academy Press. Also available at <http://books.nap.edu/catalog/1782.html>.

NRC. 1995. *Engineering Education: Designing an Adaptive System.* Washington, DC: National Academy Press. Also available at <http://books.nap.edu/catalog/4907.html>.

NRC. 1996a. *National Science Education Standards.* Washington, DC: National Academy Press. Also available at <http://books.nap.edu/catalog/4962.htmll>.

NRC. 1996b. "The Preparation of Teachers of Mathematics: Considerations and Challenges. A Letter Report from the Mathematical Sciences Education Board." (MSEB) Washington, DC: MSEB.

NRC. 1997a. *Improving Teacher Preparation and Credentialing Consistent with the* National Science Education Standards*: Report of a Symposium.* Washington, DC: National Academy Press. Also available at <http://books.nap.edu/catalog/5592.html>.

NRC. 1997b. *Science Teacher Preparation in an Era of Standards-Based Reform.* Washington, DC: National Academy Press. Also available at <http://books.nap.edu/catalog/9078.html>.

NRC. 1997c. *Science Teaching Reconsidered: A Handbook.* Washington, DC: National Academy Press. Also available at <http://books.nap.edu/catalog/5287.html>.

NRC. 1998. *Developing a Digital National Library for Undergraduate Science, Mathematics, Engineering, and Technology Education.* Washington, DC: National Academy Press. Also available at <http://books.nap.edu/catalog/5952.html>.

NRC. 1999a. *Being Fluent with Information Technology.* Washington, DC: National Academy Press. Also available at <http://books.nap.edu/catalog/6482.html>.

NRC. 1999b. *The Changing Nature of Work: Implications for Occupational Analysis.* Washington, DC: National Academy Press. Also available at <http://books.nap.edu/catalog/9600.html>.

NRC. 1999c. *Global Perspectives for Local Action: Using TIMSS to Improve U.S. Mathematics and Science Education.* Washington, DC: National Academy Press. Also available at <http://books.nap.edu/catalog/9605.html>.

NRC. 1999d. *How People Learn: Brain, Mind,*

Experience, and School. Bransford, John D., Brown, Ann L., and Cocking, Rodney R. (eds.). Washington, DC: National Academy Press. Also available at <http://books.nap.edu/catalog/6160.html>.

NRC. 1999e. *How People Learn: Bridging Research and Practice.* Donovan, M.S., Bransford, J.D., and Pellegrino, J.W. (eds.). Washington, DC: National Academy Press. Also available at <http://books.nap.edu/catalog/9457.html>.

NRC. 1999f. *Improving Student Learning: A Strategic Plan for Education Research and Its Utilization.* Washington, DC: National Academy Press. Also available at <http://books.nap.edu/catalog/6488.html>.

NRC. 1999g. *Serving the Needs of Pre-College Science and Mathematics Education: Impact of a Digital National Library on Teacher Education and Practice. Proceedings from a National Research Council Workshop.* Washington, DC: National Academy Press. Also available at <http://books.nap.edu/catalog/9584.html>.

NRC. 1999h. *Transforming Undergraduate Education in Science, Mathematics, Engineering, and Technology.* Washington, DC: National Academy Press. Also available at <http://books.nap.edu/catalog/6453.html>.

NRC. 2000a. *Inquiry and the* National Science Education Standards*: A Guide for Teaching and Learning.* Washington, DC: National Academy Press. Also available at <http://books.nap.edu/catalog/9596.html>.

NRC. 2000b. *Knowing and Learning Mathematics for Teaching: Proceedings of a Workshop.* Washington, DC: National Academy Press.

National Science Board (NSB). 1999. "Preparing our children: math and science education in the national interest." NSB 99-31. Arlington, VA: National Science Foundation. Also available at <http://www.nsf.gov/nsb/documents/1999/nsb9931/nsb9931.htm>.

National Science Foundation (NSF). 1996. *Shaping the Future: New Expectations for Undergraduate Education in Science, Mathematics, Engineering, and Technology.* Arlington, VA: National Science Foundation. Also available at <http://www.nsf.gov/cgi-bin/getpub?nsf96139>.

NSF. 1998. *Investing in Tomorrow's Teachers: The Integral Role of Two-Year Colleges in the Science and Mathematics Preparation of Prospective*

Teachers. Report from a National Science Foundation Workshop. NSF-9949. Arlington, VA: Author. Also available at <http://www.nsf.gov/cgi-bin/getpub?nsf9949>.

NSF. 2000. National Science, Mathematics, Engineering, and Technology Education Digital Library (NSDL)—Program Solicitation. Arlington, VA: Author. Available at <http://www.nsf.gov/cgi-bin/getpub?nsf0044>.

National Science Teachers Association (NSTA). 1996. *A Framework for High School Science Education.* Arlington, VA: Author. Additional information is available at <http://www.nsta.org/store/fromoutside.asp?prodnum=PB132X>.

NSTA. 1998. *NSTA Standards for Science Teacher Preparation.* Arlington, VA: Author.

NSTA. 2000. "Science Teacher Credentials, Assignments, and Job Satisfaction: Results of a Survey." Arlington, VA: Author. Also available at <http://www.nsta.org/pressrel/survey2000.asp>.

Neuschatz, M., and McFarling, M. 1999. *Maintaining Momentum: High School Physics for a New Millennium.* College Park, MD: American Institute of Physics. Report #R-427. Also available at <https://webster.aip.org/forms/statorder.htm>

Newmann, F., and Wehlage, G. 1995. *Successful School Restructuring.* Madison, WI: Center on Organization and Restructuring Schools, University of Wisconsin.

North Central Regional Educational Laboratory. 1999. "Teacher Salary and Reward Strategies." Oak Brook, IL: Author. Available at <http://www.ncrel.org/sdrs/areas/issues/envrnmnt/go/go3sal.htm>.

Odden, A. 2000. "New and better forms of teacher compensation are possible." *Phi Delta Kappan* 81(5): 361-366.

Odden, A., and Kelley, C. 1997. *Paying Teachers for What They Know and Do: New and Smarter Compensation Strategies to Improve Schools.* Thousand Oaks, CA: Corwin Press.

Olebe, M., Jackson, A., and Danielson, C. 1999. "Investing in beginning teachers: The California model." *Educational Leadership* 56(8): 41-44.

Olson, L. 1999. "Pay-performance link in salaries gains momentum." *Education Week* 19(7): 1 and 18. Also available at <http://www.edweek.com/ew/ewstory.cfm?slug=07pay.h19&keywords=Olson>.

Public Agenda. 2000. *A Sense of Calling: Who Teaches and Why.* New York: Author. Also available at <http://www.publicagenda.org/specials/teachers/teachers.htm>.

Raizen, S.A., and Michelsohn, A.M. 1994. *The Future of Science in Elementary Schools: Educating Prospective Teachers.* The National Center for Improving Science Education. San Francisco: Jossey-Bass.

Resnick, L.B., and Hall, M.W. 1998. "Learning organizations for sustainable education reform." *Daedalus* 127(4): 89-118.

Richardson, S.W. 1994. *The Professional Development School: A Common Sense Approach to Improving Education.* Forth Worth, TX: Said W. Richardson Foundation.

Rigden, D.W. 1996. "What Teachers Have to Say about Teacher Education." Washington, DC: Council for Basic Education.

Riley, R.W. 1998. "An end to quiet backwaters: Universities must make teacher education a much higher day-to-day priority." Speech given at the National Press Club. Reprinted in *Chronicle of Higher Education* 45(5), B10.

Riley, R.W. 2000. "Setting new expectations." Seventh Annual State of American Education Address, February 22, 2000, Durham, NC. Available at <http://www.ed.gov/Speeches/02-2000/000222.html>.

Rodriguez, E.M. 1998. *Preparing Quality Teachers: Issues and Trends in the States.* Washington, DC: State Higher Education Executive Officers.

Romberg, T.A. (1994). "School Mathematics: Options for the 1990s (Volume 1)." Chairman's report of a conference. Washington, DC: Office of Educational Research and Improvement, U.S. Department of Education.

Rothman, F., and Narum, J. 1999. "Then, Now, and in the Next Decade: A Commentary on Strengthening Undergraduate Science, Mathematics, Engineering, and Technology Education." Washington, DC: Project Kaleidoscope.

Rust, E. 1998. "Business Cares about Math and Science Achievement." In Business Coalition for Education Reform, *The Formula for Success: A Business Leader's Guide to Supporting Math and Science Achievement.* Washington, DC: National Alliance for Business. pp. 11-14.

Sanders, W.L., and Rivers, J.C. 1996. *Cumulative and Residual Effects of Teachers on Future Student Academic Achievement.* Knoxville, TN: University of Tennessee Value-Added Research and Assessment Center.

Schempp, P.G., Tan, S., Manross, D., and Fincher, M. 1998. "Differences in novice and competent teachers' knowledge." *Teachers and Teaching: Theory and Practice.* 4(1): 9-20.

Schon, D.A. 1983. *The Reflective Practitioner: How Professionals Think in Action.* New York: Basic Books.

Schon, D. 1987. *Educating the Reflective Practitioner.* San Francisco: Jossey-Bass.

Schon, D. 1988. "Coaching Reflective Teaching." In Grimmett, P.P., and Erickson, G.L. (eds.) *Reflection in Teacher Education.* New York: Teachers College Press.

Seymour, E., and Hewitt, N.M. 1997. *Talking About Leaving: Why Undergraduates Leave the Sciences.* Boulder, CO: Westview Press.

Shields, P.M., Esch, C., Humphrey, D.C., Young, V.M., Gaston, M., and Hunt, H. 1999. *The Status of the Teaching Profession: Research Findings and Policy Recommendations. A Report to the Teaching and California's Future Task Force.* Santa Cruz, CA: The Center for the Future of Teaching and Learning.

Shulman, L. 1986. "Those who understand: Knowledge growth in teaching." *Educational Researcher* 15,4-14.

Shulman, L. 1987. "Knowledge and teaching: Foundations of the new reform." *Harvard Educational Review* 57,1-22.

Shulman, L., and Grossman, P. 1988. "Knowledge growth in teaching: A final report to the Spencer Foundation." Stanford, CA: Stanford University.

Shroyer, M.G., Wright, E.L. and Ramey-Gassert, L. 1996. "An innovative model for collaborative reform in elementary school science reform." *Journal of Science Teacher Education* 7(3): 151-168.

Silverstein, S.C. 2000. "Impact of Teacher Participation in Columbia University's *Summer Research Program for Science Teachers* on Interest and Achievement of Their Students in Science: A Preliminary Report." Paper presented at the annual meeting of the American Society for Cell Biology, Washington, DC, December 15, 1999.

Smith, M.S., and O'Day, J. 1991. "Systemic School Reform." In Fuhrman, S. and Malen, B. (eds.). *Politics of Curriculum and Testing: The*

1990 Yearbook of the Politics of Education Association, London: Falmer. pp. 233-267.

Snyder, J. 2000. "Knowing Children—Understanding Teaching: The Developmental Teacher Education Program at the University of California-Berkeley." In Darling-Hammond, L. (ed.), *Studies of Excellence in Teacher Education: Preparation at the Graduate Level.* Washington, DC: American Association of Colleges for Teacher Education. pp. 97-172.

Sparks, D., and Hirsh, S. 2000. "A National Plan for Improving Professional Development." Oxford, OH: National Staff Development Council. Report is available on-line at <http://www.nsdc.org/library/NSDCPlan.html>.

Steinberg, R., Haymore, J. and Marks, R. 1985. "Teachers' knowledge and structuring content in mathematics." Paper presented at the meeting of the American Educational Research Association, April 1985, Chicago.

Stigler, J.W., and Hiebert, J. 1997. "Understanding and improving classroom mathematics instruction." *Phi Delta Kappan* 79: 14-21.

Stigler, J.W., and Hiebert, J. 1999. *The Teaching Gap.* New York: The Free Press.

Stoddart, T., and Floden, R.W. 1995. "Traditional and alternative routes to teacher certification: issues, assumptions, and misconceptions. "In Zeichner, K. (ed.). *Reforming Teacher Education in the United States.* New York: Teachers College Press.

Trachtman, R. 1996. The NCATE professional development school study: A survey of 28 PDS sites. Unpublished manuscript. (Available from Professional Development School Standards Project, National Council for Accreditation of Teacher Education, Washington, DC 20036.

Urban Teacher Collaborative. 2000. *The Urban Teacher Challenge: Teacher Demand and Supply in the Great City Schools.* Belmont, MA: Recruiting New Teachers, Council of the Great City Schools, Council of the Great City Colleges of Education. Also available at <http://www.rnt.org/quick/new.html>.

U.S. Department of Education. 1996. National Center for Education Statistics. *Pursuing Excellence.* NCES 97-198. Washington, DC: U.S. Government Printing Office. See also <http://www.ed.gov/NCES/timss>.

U.S. Department of Education. 1997a. National Center for Education Statistics. *America's Teachers: Profile of a Profession, 1993-94.* NCES 97-460. Washington, DC: National Center for Education Statistics.

U.S. Department of Education. 1997b. National Center for Education Statistics. *Digest of Education Statistics.* NCES 98-015. Washington, DC: National Center for Education Statistics. See also <http://nces.ed.gov/pubsearch/pubsinfo.asp?pubid=2000031>.

U.S. Department of Education. 1999. National Center for Education Statistics. *Digest of Education Statistics.* Washington, DC: National Center for Education Statistics. See also <http://nces.ed.gov/pubsearch/pubsinfo.asp?pubid=2000031>.

Valdez, G., McNabb, M., Foertsch, M., Anderson, M., Hawkes, M., and Raack, L. 1999. *Computer-Based Technology and Learning: Evolving Uses and Expectations.* Oak Brook, IL: North Central Regional Educational Laboratory. Available at <http://www.ncrel.org/tplan/cbtl/toc.htm>.

Wasley, P. 1999. "Teaching worth celebrating." *Educational Leadership* 56(8): 8-13.

Whitford, B.L., and Metcalf-Turner, P. 1999. "Of promises and unresolved puzzles: Reforming teacher education through Professional Development Schools." In Griffin, G.A. (ed.), *The Education of Teachers: Ninety-eighth Yearbook of the National Society for the Study of Education.* Chicago: University of Chicago Press. pp. 257-278.

Whitford, B.L., Ruscoe, G., and Fickel, L. 2000. "Knitting It All Together: Collaborative Teacher Education in Southern Maine." In: Darling-Hammond, L. (ed.). *Studies of Excellence in Teacher Education: Preparation at the Graduate Level.* Washington, DC: American Association of Colleges for Teacher Education. pp. 173-257.

Wiley, D., and Yoon, B. 1995. "Teacher Reports of Opportunity to Learn: Analyses of the 1993 California Learning Assessment System." *Educational Evaluation and Policy Analysis* 17(3): 355-370.

Wilson, S.M., Shulman L.S., and Richert, A.E. 1987. "150 different ways of knowing: Representation of knowing in teaching." In Calderhead, J. (ed.), *Exploring Teachers' Thinking.* London: Cassell. pp. 104-124.

Wright, S.P., Horn, S.P., and Sanders, W.L. 1997. "Teacher and classroom context effects on student achievement: implications for teacher evaluation." *Journal of Personnel Evaluation in Education* 11: 57-67.

Yates, A. 1995. "Higher education has a link to real reform at the K-12 level." *The Denver Post*, April 29, 8b.

Zeichner, K. 2000. "Ability-Based Teacher Education: Elementary Teacher Education at Alverno College." In Darling-Hammond, L. (ed.), *Studies of Excellence in Teacher Education: Preparation in the Undergraduate Years.* Washington, DC: American Association of Colleges for Teacher Education. pp. 1-66.

Appendix A
Standards for Teacher Development and Professional Conduct

From the *National Science Education Standards*

(National Research Council, 1996a; excerpted from pages 55-73)

PROFESSIONAL DEVELOPMENT

STANDARD A:

Professional development for teachers of science requires learning essential science content through the perspectives and methods of inquiry. Science learning experiences for teachers must

- Involve teachers in actively investigating phenomena that can be studied scientifically, interpreting results, and making sense of findings consistent with currently accepted scientific understanding.

- Address issues, events, problems, or topics significant in science and of interest to participants.
- Introduce teachers to scientific literature, media, and technological resources that expand their science knowledge and their ability to access further knowledge.
- Build on the teacher's current science understanding, ability, and attitudes.
- Incorporate ongoing reflection on the process and outcomes of understanding science through inquiry.
- Encourage and support teachers in efforts to collaborate.

STANDARD B:

Professional development for teachers of science requires integrating knowledge of science, learning, pedagogy, and students; it also requires applying that knowledge to science teaching. Learning experiences for teachers of science must

- Connect and integrate all pertinent aspects of science and science education.
- Occur in a variety of places where effective science teaching can be illustrated and modeled, permitting teachers to struggle with real situations and expand their knowledge and skills in appropriate contexts.
- Address teachers' needs as learners and build on their current knowledge of science content, teaching, and learning.
- Use inquiry, reflection, interpretation of research, modeling, and guided practice to build understanding and skill in science teaching.

STANDARD C:

Professional development for teachers of science requires building understanding and ability for lifelong learning. Professional development activities must

- Provide regular, frequent opportunities for individual and collegial examination and reflection on classroom and institutional practice.
- Provide opportunities for teachers to receive feedback about their teaching and to understand, analyze, and apply that feedback to improve their practice.
- Provide opportunities for teachers to learn and use various tools and techniques for self-reflection and

collegial reflection, such as peer coaching, portfolios, and journals.
- Support the sharing of teacher expertise by preparing and using mentors, teacher advisers, coaches, lead teachers, and resource teachers to provide professional development opportunities.
- Provide opportunities to know and have access to existing research and experiential knowledge.
- Provide opportunities to learn and use the skills of research to generate new knowledge about science and the teaching and learning of science.

STANDARD D:

Professional development programs for teachers of science must be coherent and integrated. Quality preservice and inservice programs are characterized by

- Clear, shared goals based on a vision of science learning, teaching, and teacher development congruent with the *National Science Education Standards*.
- Integration and coordination of the program components so that understanding and ability can be built over time, reinforced continuously, and practiced in a variety of situations.
- Options that recognize the developmental nature of teacher professional growth and individual and group

interest, as well as the need of teachers who have varying degrees of experience, professional expertise, and proficiency.

- Collaboration among the people involved in programs, including teachers, teacher educators, teacher unions, scientists, administrators, policy makers, members of professional and scientific organizations, parents, and business people, with clear respect for the perspectives and expertise of each.
- Recognition of the history, culture, and organization of the school environment.
- Continuous program assessment that captures the perspectives of all those involved, uses a variety of strategies, focuses on the process and effects of the program, and feeds directly into program improvement and evaluation.

From the NCTM *Standards for the Professional Development of Teachers of Mathematics*

(National Council of Teachers of Mathematics, 1991, excerpted from pages 127-173)

Standard 1. Experiencing Good Mathematics Teaching

Mathematics and mathematics education instructors in preservice and continuing education programs should model good mathematics teaching by—

- Posing worthwhile mathematical tasks;
- Engaging teachers in mathematical discourse;
- Enhancing mathematical discourse through the use of a variety of tools, including calculators, computers, and physical and pictorial models;
- Creating learning environments that support and encourage mathematical reasoning and teachers' dispositions and abilities to do mathematics;
- Expecting and encouraging teachers to take intellectual risks in doing mathematics and to work independently and collaboratively;
- Representing mathematics as an ongoing human activity
- Affirming and supporting full participation and continued study of mathematics by all students.

Standard 2. Knowing Mathematics and School Mathematics

The education of teachers of mathematics should develop their knowledge of the content and discourse of mathematics, including—

- Mathematical concepts and procedures and the connections among them;
- Multiple representations of mathematical concepts and procedures;
- Ways to reason mathematically, solve

problems, and communicate mathematics effectively at different levels of formality;

And, in addition develop their perspectives on—

- The nature of mathematics, the contributions of different cultures toward the development of mathematics, and the role of mathematics in culture and society;
- The changes in the nature of mathematics and the way we teach, learn, and do mathematics resulting from the availability of technology;
- School mathematics within the discipline of mathematics;
- The changing nature of school mathematics, its relationships to other school subjects, and its applications in society.

Standard 3. Knowing Students as Learners of Mathematics

The preservice and continuing education of teachers of mathematics should provide multiple perspectives on students as learners of mathematics by developing teachers' knowledge of—

- Research on how students learn mathematics;
- The effects of students' age, abilities, interests, and experience on learning mathematics;

- The influences of students' linguistic, ethnic, racial, and socioeconomic backgrounds and gender on learning mathematics;
- Ways to affirm and support full participation and continued study of mathematics by all students.

Standard 4. Knowing Mathematical Pedagogy

The preservice and continuing education of teachers of mathematics should develop teachers' knowledge of and ability to use and evaluate—

- Instructional materials and resources, including technology;
- Ways to represent mathematics concepts and procedures;
- Instructional strategies and classroom organizational models;
- Ways to promote discourse and foster a sense of mathematical community;
- Means for assessing student understanding of mathematics.

Standard 5. Developing as a Teacher of Mathematics

The preservice and continuing education of teachers of mathematics should provide them with opportunities to—

- Examine and revise their assumptions about the nature of mathematics, how it should be taught, and how students learn mathematics;

- Observe and analyze a range of approaches to mathematics teaching and learning, focusing on the tasks, discourse, environment, and assessment;
- Work with a diverse range of students individually, in small groups, and in large class settings with guidance from and in collaboration with mathematics education professionals;
- Analyze and evaluate the appropriateness and effectiveness of their teaching;
- Develop dispositions toward teaching mathematics.

Standard 6. The Teacher's Role in Professional Development

Teachers of mathematics should take an active role in their own professional development by accepting responsibility for—

- Experimenting thoughtfully with alternative approaches and strategies in the classroom;
- Reflecting on learning and teaching individually and with colleagues;
- Participating in workshop, courses, and other educational opportunities specific to mathematics;
- Participating actively in the professional community of mathematics educators;
- Reading and discussing ideas presented in professional publications;
- Discussing with colleagues issues in mathematics and mathematics teaching and learning;
- Participating in proposing, designing, and evaluating programs for professional development specific to mathematics;
- Participating in school, community, and political efforts to effect positive change in mathematics education.

Schools and school districts must support and encourage teachers in accepting these responsibilities.

Appendix B
Overview of Content Standards from the *National Science Education Standards* and the *Principles and Standards for School Mathematics*

Science Content Standards for Grades K-12

(From the *National Science Education Standards,* National Research Council, 1996a, excerpted from pages 103-119)

RATIONALE

The eight categories of content standards are

- Unifying concepts and processes in science
- Science as inquiry
- Physical science
- Life science
- Earth and space science
- Science and technology
- Science in personal and social perspectives
- History and nature of science

Unifying Concepts and Processes Standard

Unifying concepts and processes include

- Systems, order, and organization
- Evidence, models, and explanation
- Change, constancy, and measurement
- Evolution and equilibrium
- Form and function

Science as Inquiry Standards

Engaging students in inquiry helps students develop

- Understanding of scientific concepts
- An appreciation of "how we know" what we know in science
- Understanding of the nature of science
- Skills necessary to become independent inquirers about the natural world
- The dispositions to use the skills,

abilities, and attitudes associated with science

Physical Science, Life Science, and Earth and Space Science Standards

The standards for physical science, life science, and earth and space science describe the subject matter of science using three widely accepted divisions of the domain of science. Science subject matter focuses on the science facts, concepts, principles, theories, and models that are important for all students to know, understand, and use.

Science and Technology Standards

The science and technology standards establish connections between the natural and designed worlds and provide students with opportunities to develop decision-making abilities. They are not standards for technology education; rather, these standards emphasize abilities associated with the process of design and fundamental understandings about the enterprise of science and its various linkages with technology.

Science in Personal and Social Perspectives Standards

An important purpose of science education is to give students a means to understand and act on personal and social issues. The science in personal

and social perspectives standards help students develop decision-making skills. Understandings associated with these concepts give students a foundation on which to base decisions they will face as citizens.

History and Nature of Science Standards

In learning science, students need to understand that science reflects its history and is an ongoing, changing enterprise. The standards for the history and nature of science recommend the use of history in school science programs to clarify different aspects of scientific inquiry, the human aspects of science, and the role that science has played in the development of various cultures.

FORM OF THE CONTENT STANDARDS

Below is an example of a content standard.

Physical Science (Example)

As a result of the activities in grades K-4, all students should develop an understanding of

- Properties of objects and materials
- Position and motion of objects
- Light, heat, electricity, and magnetism

Content is fundamental if it

- Represents a central event or phenomenon in the natural world.
- Represents a central scientific idea and organizing principle.
- Has rich explanatory power.
- Guides fruitful investigations.
- Applies to situations and contexts common to everyday experiences.
- Can be linked to meaningful learning experiences.
- Is developmentally appropriate for students at the grade level specified.

CRITERIA FOR THE CONTENT STANDARDS

Three criteria influence the selection of science content.

- The first is an obligation to the domain of science. The subject matter in the physical, life, and earth and space science standards is central to science education and must be accurate.
- The second criterion is an obligation to develop content standards that appropriately represent the development and learning abilities of students.
- The third criterion is an obligation to present standards in a usable form for those who must implement the standards.

USE OF THE CONTENT STANDARDS

Persons responsible for science curricula, teaching, assessment and policy who use the *Standards* should note the following

- None of the eight categories of content standards should be eliminated. For instance, students should have opportunities to learn science in personal and social perspectives and to learn about the history and nature of science, as well as to learn subject matter, in the school science program.
- No standards should be eliminated from a category. For instance, "biological evolution" cannot be eliminated from the life science standards.
- Science content can be added. The connections, depth, detail, and selection of topics can be enriched and varied as appropriate for individual students and school science program.
- The content standards must be used in the context of the standards on teaching and assessments. Using the standards with traditional teaching and assessment strategies defeats the intentions of the *National Science Education Standards*.

Mathematics Content Standards for Grades K-12

(From National Council of Teachers of Mathematics, 2000, excerpted from pages 28-71)

PREKINDERGARTEN THROUGH GRADE 12[1]

Number and Operations Standard

Instructional programs from prekindergarten through grade 12 should enable all students to—

- Understand numbers, ways of representing numbers, relationships among numbers, and number systems;
- Understand meanings of operations and how they relate to one another;
- Compute fluently and make reasonable estimates.

Algebra Standard

Instructional programs from prekindergarten through grade 12 should enable all students to—

- Understand patterns, relations, and functions;

- Represent and analyze mathematical situations and structures using algebraic symbols;
- Use mathematical models to represent and understand quantitative relationships;
- Analyze change in various contexts.

Geometry Standard

Instructional programs from prekindergarten through grade 12 should enable all students to—

- Analyze characteristics and properties of two- and three-dimensional geometric shapes and develop mathematical arguments about geometric relationships;
- Specify locations and describe spatial relationships using coordinate geometry and other representational systems;
- Apply transformations and use symmetry to analyze mathematical situations;
- Use visualization, spatial reasoning, and geometric modeling to solve problems.

Measurement Standard

Instructional programs from prekindergarten through grade 12 should enable all students to—

---

[1]Excerpted from National Council of Teachers of Mathematics (2000) pages 29-71.

- Understand measurable attributes of objects and the units, systems, and processes of measurement;
- Apply appropriate techniques, tools, and formulas to determine measurements.

Data Analysis and Probability Standard

Instructional programs from prekindergarten through grade 12 should enable all students to—

- Formulate questions that can be addressed with data and collect, organize, and display relevant data to answer them;
- Select and use appropriate statistical methods to analyze data;
- Develop and evaluate inferences and predictions that are based on data;
- Understand and apply basic concepts of probability.

Problem Solving Standard

Instructional programs from prekindergarten through grade 12 should enable all students to—

- Build new mathematical knowledge through problem solving;
- Solve problems that arise in mathematics and in other contexts;
- Apply and adapt a variety of appropri-

ate strategies to solve problems;
- Monitor and reflect on the process of mathematical problem solving.

Reasoning and Proof Standard

Instructional programs from prekindergarten through grade 12 should enable all students to—

- Recognize reasoning and proof as fundamental aspects of mathematics;
- Make and investigate mathematical conjectures;
- Develop and evaluate mathematical arguments and proofs;
- Select and use various types of reasoning and methods of proof.

Communication Standard

Instructional programs from prekindergarten through grade 12 should enable all students to—

- Organize and consolidate their mathematical thinking through communication;
- Communicate their mathematical thinking coherently and clearly to peers, teachers, and others;
- Analyze and evaluate the mathematical thinking and strategies of others;
- Use the language of mathematics to express mathematical ideas precisely.

Connections Standard

Instructional programs from prekindergarten through grade 12 should enable all students to—

- Recognize and use connections among mathematical ideas;
- Understand how mathematical ideas interconnect and build on one another to produce a coherent whole;
- Recognize and apply mathematics in contexts outside of mathematics.

Representation Standard

Instructional programs from prekindergarten through grade 12 should enable all students to—

- Create and use representations to organize, record, and communicate mathematical ideas;
- Select, apply, and translate among mathematical representations to solve problems;
- Use representations to model and interpret physical, social, and mathematical phenomena.

Appendix C
Overview of Teaching Standards from the *National Science Education Standards* and the *Principles and Standards for School Mathematics*

Science Teaching Standards

(From the *National Science Education Standards*, National Research Council, 1996a, excerpted from pages 27-53)

The standards for science teaching are grounded in five assumptions.

- The vision of science education described by the *Standards* requires changes throughout the entire system.
- What students learn is greatly influenced by how they are taught.
- The actions of teachers are deeply influenced by their perceptions of science as an enterprise and as a subject to be taught and learned.
- Student understanding is actively constructed through individual and social processes.
- Actions of teachers are deeply influenced by their understanding of and relationships with students.

TEACHING STANDARD A:

Teachers of science plan an inquiry-based science program for their students. In doing this, teachers

- Develop a framework of yearlong and short-term goals for students.
- Select science content and adapt and design curricula to meet the interest, knowledge, understanding, abilities, and experiences of students.
- Select teaching and assessment strategies that support the development of student understanding and nurture a community of science learners.
- Work together as colleagues within and across disciplines and grade levels.

TEACHING STANDARD B:

Teachers of science guide and facilitate learning. In doing this, teachers

- Focus and support inquiries while interacting with students.
- Orchestrate discourse among students about scientific ideas.
- Challenge students to accept and share responsibility for their own learning.
- Recognize and respond to student diversity and encourage all students to participate fully in science learning.
- Encourage and model the skills of scientific inquiry, as well as the curiosity, openness to new ideas and data, and skepticism that characterize science.

TEACHING STANDARD C:

Teachers of science engage in ongoing assessment of their teaching and of student learning. In doing this, teachers

- Use multiple methods and systematically gather data about student understanding and ability.
- Analyze assessment data to guide teaching.
- Guide students in self-assessment.
- Use student data, observations of teaching, and interactions with colleagues to reflect on and improve teaching practice.
- Use student data, observations of teaching, and interactions with colleagues to report student achievement and opportunities to learn to students, teachers, parents, policy makers, and the general public.

TEACHING STANDARD D:

Teachers of science design and manage learning environments that provide students with the time, space, and resources needed for learning science. In doing this, teachers

- Structure the time available so that students are able to engage in extended investigations.
- Create a setting for student work that is flexible and supportive of science inquiry.
- Ensure a safe working environment.
- Make the available science tools, materials, media, and technological resources accessible to students.
- Identify and use resources outside the school.
- Engage students in designing the learning environment.

TEACHING STANDARD E:

Teachers of science develop communities of science learners that reflect the intellectual rigor of scientific inquiry and the attitudes and social values conducive to science learning. In doing the, teachers

- Display and demand respect for the diverse ideas, skills, and experiences of all students.
- Enable students to have a significant voice in decisions about the content and context of their work and require

students to take responsibility for the learning of all members of the community.

- Nurture collaboration among students.
- Structure and facilitate ongoing formal and informal discussion based on a shared understanding of rules of scientific discourse.
- Model and emphasize the skills, attitudes, and values of scientific inquiry.

TEACHING STANDARD F:

Teachers of science actively participate in the ongoing planning and development of the school science program. In doing this, teachers

- Plan and develop the school science program.
- Participate in decisions concerning the allocation of time and other resources to the science program.
- Participate fully in planning and implementing professional growth and development strategies for themselves and their colleagues.

From the *Principles and Standards for School Mathematics*

(National Council of Teachers of Mathematics, 2000, excerpted from pages 25-67).

Standard 1. Worthwhile Mathematical Tasks

The teacher of mathematics should pose tasks that are based on—

- Sound and significant mathematics;
- Knowledge of students' understandings, interests, and experiences;
- Knowledge of the range of ways that diverse students learn mathematics;

And that

- Engage students' intellect;
- Develop students' mathematical understandings and skills;
- Stimulate students to make connections and develop a coherent framework for mathematical ideas;
- Call for problem formulation, problem solving, and mathematical reasoning;
- Promote communication about mathematics;
- Represent mathematics as an ongoing human activity;
- Display sensitivity to, and draw on, students' diverse background experiences and dispositions;
- Promote the development of all students' dispositions to do mathematics

Standard 2. The Teacher's Role in Discourse

The teacher of mathematics should orchestrate discourse by—

- Posing questions and tasks that elicit, engage, and challenge each student's thinking;
- Listening carefully to students' ideas;
- Asking students to clarify and justify their ideas orally and in writing;
- Deciding what to pursue in depth from among the ideas that students bring up during a discussion;
- Deciding when and how to attach mathematical notation and language to students' ideas;
- Deciding when to provide information, when to clarify and issue, when to model, when to lead, and when to let a student struggle with a difficulty;
- Monitoring students' participation in discussions and deciding when and how to encourage each student to participate.

Standard 3. Students' Role in Discourse

The teacher of mathematics should promote classroom discourse in which students—

- Listen to, respond to, and question the teacher and one another;
- Use a variety of tools to reason, make connections, solve problems, and communicate;
- Initiate problems and question;
- Make conjectures and present solutions;

- Explore examples and counter-examples to investigate a conjecture;
- Try to convince themselves and one another of the validity of particular representations, solutions, conjectures, and answers;
- Rely on mathematical evidence and argument to determine validity.

Standard 4. Tools for Enhancing Discourse

The teacher of mathematics, in order to enhance discourse, should encourage and accept the use of—

- Computers, calculators, and other technology;
- Concrete materials used as models;
- Pictures, diagrams, tables, and graphs;
- Invented and conventional terms and symbols
- Metaphors, analogies, and stories;
- Written hypotheses, explanations, and arguments;
- Oral presentations and dramatizations.

Standard 5. Learning Environment

The teacher of mathematics should create a learning environment that fosters the development of each student's mathematical power by—

- Providing and structuring the time necessary to explore sound mathematics and grapple with significant ideas and problems;
- Using the physical space and materials in ways that facilitate students' learning of mathematics;
- Providing a context that encourages the development of mathematical dispositions;

And by consistently expecting and encouraging students to—

- Work independently or collaboratively to make sense of mathematics;
- Take intellectual risks by raising questions and formulating conjectures;
- Display a sense of mathematical competence by validating and supporting ideas with mathematical argument.

Standard 6. Analysis of Teaching and Learning

The teacher of mathematics should engage in ongoing analysis of teaching and learning by—

- Observing, listening to, and gathering other information about students to assess what they are learning;
- Examining effects of the tasks, discourse, and learning environment on students' mathematical knowledge, skills, and dispositions;

In order to—

- Ensure that every student is learning sound and significant mathematics and is developing a positive disposition toward mathematics;
- Challenge and extend students' ideas;
- Adapt or change activities while teaching; make plans, both short- and long-range;
- Describe and comment on each student's learning to parents and administrators, as well as to the students themselves.

Appendix D
Examples of Local and Statewide Programs That Provide Ongoing Professional Development Opportunities to Beginning and Experienced Teachers

Note: The examples provided in this appendix are included to provide readers with an appreciation for the breadth and variety of current programs. They are not intended to provide detailed case studies. See footnotes for URLs for further information.

CALIFORNIA BEGINNING TEACHER SUPPORT AND ASSESSMENT SYSTEM[1]

A longitudinal study conducted in California has found that the most effective approaches for supporting new teachers emphasize optimizing the relationship between new teachers and teachers who provide support and mentoring to them (Halford, 1998). As

a result, California has instituted the Beginning Teacher Support and Assessment System for first- and second- year teachers, which involves an extensive and systematic mentoring program for new teachers by their more experienced colleagues. For example, mentors work with new teachers to develop lesson plans that are based on the state's standards for teaching.

TEACHERS 21[2]

At the national level, Teachers 21 and its affiliate organization, Research for Better Teaching, are dedicated to strengthening the practice of teaching for both new and experienced teachers. These not-for-profit organizations also

---

[1]Additional information about this program is available at < http://www.cccoe.k12.ca.us/coe/curins/sbtsa/>.

[2]Additional information about this program is available at < http://www.teachers21.org/>.

are working to help administrators become more involved in systemic improvements in schools.

Teachers 21 features ongoing seminars and courses that train beginning teachers to network, build partnerships with parents, engage in positive classroom management, link curriculum and assessment to curriculum frameworks, and explore ranges of pedagogical approaches to teaching science and mathematics. This organization also works to establish support groups for beginning teachers that focus on professional growth. These support groups meet on a regular basis throughout the year and help novice teachers reflect on their teaching and on their students' learning.

Another key component to the success of the approach by Teachers 21 is the training of mentors. The third element is including principals and other administrators in all phases of the programs. In addition, Teachers 21 commits to building school culture that engage school administrators, new and veteran teachers, and others in the community in improving schools.

Teachers 21 maintains that the districts it considers progressive are those that care about both the professional growth of their teachers and the quality of their teaching. According to

Teachers 21, the success of beginning teachers depends on the support of everyone in a school. Structures, time, space, and the availability of collegial practice that support observations, joint lesson planning, and curriculum development are important components to the success of new teachers. The organization further contends that such plans must be embraced and publicized by districts in order to ensure that mentoring programs are seen as vital to the community.

BOSTON PLAN FOR EXCELLENCE IN THE PUBLIC SCHOOLS[3]

On a district level, the City of Boston has developed a five- year, $5-million program called The Boston Plan for Excellence in the Public Schools. Now in its third year, this program combines and integrates improved professional preparation of its teachers with programs to raise academic achievement of its students. Twenty-five schools are currently involved. Key components of this program include:

- Provision of an on-site coach for teacher professional development
- One day per week in each school for these programs

---

[3]Additional information about this program is available at < http://www.bpe.org/>.

- Creation of and instructional leadership team in each school
- Decision-making by cluster groups of teachers
- Liaisons to each school made up of retired principals, teacher-consultants, and others
- On-site workshops for teachers

NOTE: The following examples are from states that entered into partnership with the *National Commission on Teaching and America's Future* (1997) and demonstrate the range of approaches that can impact on teacher development and preparation.

NORTH CAROLINA UNIVERSITY-SCHOOL TEACHER EDUCATION PARTNERSHIPS [4]

Three years ago, North Carolina established the University-School Teacher Education Partnerships, an initiative that will create "clinical schools" for novice and veteran teachers at all of the 15 public teacher education institutions in that state. Many of these universities also are planning to establish more elaborate Professional Development Schools. These partnerships are operated based on five guiding principles:

1. increased time for preservice teachers to experience earlier, longer, and more intensive field-based placements in the public schools, connected to methods classes and clinical teachers at school sites;
2. jointly-crafted professional development programs for teachers, administrators, and others in the public schools and universities;
3. increased communication between public schools and higher education for the purpose of sharing and disseminating best practices;
4. generation and application of research and new knowledge about teaching and learning;
5. joint involvement of university and school personnel in curriculum planning and program development. (quoted verbatim from Edelfelt, 1999, page 2).

OHIO'S PROGRAM FOR TEACHER EDUCATION

Since September 1996, Ohio has had in place through its association with the National Commission on Teaching and America's Future, a "comprehensive new infrastructure for preparing, licensing, and promoting the professional development of teachers." Within this

---

[4]Additional information about this program is available at <http://www.ga.unc.edu/>.

statewide infrastructure, mentors are provided for all beginning teachers and principals. Peer review of and assistance with teaching skills are encouraged through competitive grants to school systems. In addition, funds are available to implement peer review programs and for the training of mentor teachers at regional professional development centers. The Ohio State Board of Education has authorized a waiver of its rules on teacher professional days to provide the flexibility needed to create time for professional development, and this has had beneficial effects. For example, Ohio's Centerville School District was able to negotiate with the local teachers' union to provide release time and $1,000 stipends for mentor teachers (Halford, 1998). Tangible incentives, district support, specialized professional support for mentors, and careful attention to the matches between mentors and new teachers are key components of Centerville's program.

SUPPORT FOR TEACHERS IN OKLAHOMA, MARYLAND, KANSAS, AND MISSOURI

Oklahoma has provided additional funds to its Commission for Teacher Preparation to launch professional development institutes that focus on the teaching of mathematics, the teaching of inquiry-based science, the use of technology in the classroom, and the training of mentors for beginning teachers.[5]

In Maryland, 240 new Professional Development Schools will be launched, expanding the current efforts of its 13 public universities. All prospective teachers in the state of Maryland ultimately will be expected to complete a year-long internship in connection with these PDSs (Maryland State Department of Education, 1998).

Kansas also has committed to ongoing professional development and new induction programs that hold teacher education programs accountable for the performance of their graduates. The Kansas Teacher Development Coalition,[6] a collaboration of state agencies, higher education institutions, and other educators, has been working to align preservice education and induction-related professional development with that state's redesign of teacher licensure. Meanwhile, each of six Regents institutions in Kansas has established professional development school partnerships for the clinical preparation of new teachers.

Missouri has established a Super-

[5]Additional information about these institutes is available at < http://sde.state.ok.us/pro/teach.html>.

[6]Additional information is available at < http://www.usd259.com/staff/teacher-dev-coalition.htm>.

intendents' Institute to help prepare teacher leaders become more knowledgeable about innovation, the process of change, and successful practices. New incentive grants for innovation will help schools and districts use educational research and adopt teaching practices that have been found to be successful elsewhere (NCTAF, 1997). The state also has created Professional Development Schools and is considering PDS standards, a statewide support network, and a stable funding structure of PDSs.[7]

---

[7]Additional information is available at < http://www.dese.state.mo.us/divurbteached/rpdc/>.

Appendix E
Examples of Formal and Informal Partnerships Between Institutions of Higher Education and School Districts to Improve Teacher Education

Note: The examples provided in this appendix are included to provide readers with an appreciation for the breadth and variety of current programs. These types of programs might serve as prototypes for the types of partnerships envisioned in this report (see Chapters 6 and 7). See URLs in text and in footnotes for further information.

Alverno College (Milwaukee, Wisconsin)[1] is a four-year private liberal arts college whose teacher preparation program reflects recent research about how prospective teachers should be educated. The approach includes defining clearly what candidates for licensure need to know, understand, and be able to do as teachers. Alverno's teacher education program supports a coherent curriculum, a supportive system of performance assessments,

collaboration among the various faculty of the college, and multiple forms of partnerships with the urban school system of Milwaukee. Since the inception of the program in the late 1970s, Alverno has continued to seek to link the program components and create a teacher preparation program that is based on the scholarly literature for the profession, the experiences of the college's faculty and students, and empirical studies. Tenets of the new teacher development program are based on what the faculty has come to call "assessment-as-learning." The essential characteristics of this concept are

- Candidates are aware of the expected outcomes;
- Faculty provide continuous, careful, and productive feedback to candidates based on evidence that has been

---

[1]See also <http://ww.alverno.edu/academics/departments/ac_elemented.html>.

collected about their performance;

- Students engage in self-assessment;
- Multiple measures and evidence of high performance by teacher candidates are required throughout the undergraduate curriculum.

These high expectations, in turn, cultivate communication across the disciplines at Alverno. The college also recognizes and supports this level of collaboration through its promotion and performance review systems.

In addition, Alverno has sought to bridge the gap between theory and practice by establishing partnerships with a number of schools in the Milwaukee public school system. At each partner school, Alverno students work with the K-12 staff and are guided by an Alverno faculty member. Students' work in the partner schools does not focus exclusively on meeting their own needs but, rather, is guided, in part, by the needs of the Milwaukee public school system. Several middle and high schools, for example, are learning from Alverno faculty and students how to implement the assessment-as-learning model and are engaged in research studies of the implementation of the partnership programs in their schools. Alverno does not refer to its programs

as Professional Development Schools. However, the overseers of these programs at Alverno believe that this approach to teacher education is having an impact similar to the impacts of other Professional Development Schools (Dietz, 1999; Zeichner, 2000).

Clark University-Worcester Public Schools (Worcester, Massachusetts)[2]

Clark University and the Worcester Public Schools have established a K-16 collaborative that uses a "rounds" model of professional development. The concept of "rounds" is based on the training model used in teaching hospitals. This partnership version of rounds engages small groups of school-based teachers, university teachers, and students involved with teacher education in learning together about specific aspects of teaching practice. Aspects include learning about how to implement a specific curriculum, understanding how children learn, and knowledge building in a particular context, or all of these domains of classroom activity at once. A round also might serve as a way to share and examine one's teaching practice with colleagues. During student teaching, students typically take weekly turns conducting rounds. The

---

[2]Additional information about this program is available at< www2.clarku.edu/departments/ education/>.

rounds process gives them the collective confidence to engage their own students in learning (Del Prete, 1997). The rounds also reflect a shift toward more collaborative relationships, reflective dialogue, research, and study, and a process of open, active and continuous expansion of professional knowledge on the part of the entire community (Del Prete, 1997).

Houston Consortium (Houston, Texas)

To better prepare prospective urban teachers, a consortium of four universities (University of Houston, Texas Southern University, Houston Baptist University, and University of St. Thomas), three school districts, and two intermediate school agencies designed and implemented a Professional Development School program located in several Houston area K-12 schools. The consortium has been operating for more than five years and uses twelve mutually agreed upon characteristics to guide its work, including flexibility, cultural diversity, learner-centered instruction, technology, and authentic assessment. Recently reported research on the model indicates that 43 percent of the teacher participants believe that they now teach differently, and classroom observations confirm this. Achievement levels for both the preservice candidates

and their students have increased as well (Houston et al., 1999). Data from this 1999 study indicates that the Professional Development School program preservice candidate teachers interacted with students more often than preservice candidates who were not in the program. They also spent significantly more time responding to student signals, checking student work, encouraging student self-management, praising student performance and behavior, and correcting student performance.

Kansas State University (Manhattan, Kansas)

Since 1989, Kansas State University's College of Education has been engaged in partnerships with three local school districts, establishing Professional Development Schools in twelve elementary schools, four middle schools, and one high school. The Kansas State University (KSU) PDS Model is based on the belief that teacher preparation and school reform are the joint responsibility of institutions of higher education and school systems. All teachers and principals from the 17 PDS sites are now collaborative partners. The PDS and KSU faculty members are involved with all phases of the KSU teacher preparation program. At the building level, each PDS has identified at least one clinical instructor and KSU faculty member to work with the building principal to coordinate the PDS activities and experiences. The goal is to create new roles for all PDS and KSU partners and to establish a joint community of learners. The program implements this goal by using teachers, administrators, and KSU faculty as co-planners, teachers, and evaluators of methods courses and field experiences; on-site PDS seminar leaders; and supervisors and mentors of practicing teachers. Teachers, administrators, and faculty also are jointly involved in school improvement efforts, curriculum development, program evaluation, professional development activities, and collaborative action research projects.

The project has published its results through a number of doctoral dissertations and other reports (see, for example, Shroyer et al., 1996). The project has created a climate of experimentation and risk taking that has helped build a joint culture of inquiry among PDS partners, whereby faculty and teachers constantly experiment with new ideas, evaluate teaching strategies, and revise their practices. Research indicates that this type of culture is a critical component of both successful professional development and educational improvement.

University of Massachusetts-Boston/Graham and Parks Alternative School (Cambridge, Massachusetts)

This group has been collaborating for the past five years on a professional development site. The Graham and Parks School (G&P) is diverse ethnically and racially. It has demonstrated a commitment to ongoing professional development of its staff and to involving parents in the school's mission and activities. The school administration supports an innovative, reflective attitude towards teaching and learning. The University of Massachusetts at Boston (UMB) has long espoused a commitment to its urban setting. The campus attracts a diversity of teacher candidates who reflect the range of students in the cultural makeup of the K-8 school. These two institutions selected each other as partners because of these attributes and their commitment to improving teacher education and professional development.

Over the five years of the partnership's existence, UMB has offered three on-site graduate seminars for teachers and staff, including the school principal, in which issues such as "effective teaching" and the "teaching and assessment of writing" have been evaluated. In addition to entering into graduate seminar dialogues on teaching and learning,

G&P teachers have served on overview committees for the development and revision of courses at UMB for students preparing to become elementary and middle school teachers. These committees bring together university faculty from science and mathematics departments, schools of education, and public school teachers and administrators to discuss ways to revise existing courses and design new courses in the UMB teacher preparation program.

Since the spring of 1996, six G&P teachers have been meeting monthly with UMB faculty to develop further teacher education programs for UMB students. Results include an on-site seminar at G&P, which is co-taught by the teachers and the on-site supervisor and which links the course and field-work. A G&P teacher teaches another on-site course on structured reading and special needs students. Teachers and UMB faculty also co-teach a year-long internship program that requires UMB interns to document their growth as teachers through analysis of video-taped teaching sessions and creation of teaching portfolios.

University of Texas at Austin

In 1997, the University of Texas at Austin established UTeach,[3] a program operated jointly by the College of Education (CE) and the College of Natural Resources (CNR). UTeach was designed to attract more students to science and mathematics teaching at the secondary level. The program introduces students to teaching with a one-hour course and then builds on that experience through a series of three-hour courses that culminate in a full-time commitment to teacher education. The program attracts more women and minorities than other teacher-education programs in the state of Texas and relies on close collaboration with and guidance from locally and nationally recognized master teachers. UTeach emphasizes collegiality by having entering cohorts of students work together on virtually all aspects of their education in teaching.

Students who complete the program earn a degree in science or mathematics (under the auspices of CNR) and teacher certification (through CE) at the end of four years. Students acquire initial teaching experience in public schools by giving presentations about science to elementary school children in the Austin area and then moving on to the middle- and high-school levels later in their coursework. UTeach was the first teacher preparation program in Texas to meet the state's revised standards for certification.

---

[3]Additional information about this program is available at <http://www.utexas.edu/cons/admin/publications/focus/spring99/teach.html>.

Wheelock College and Brookline Public Schools (Brookline, Massachusetts)

The Learning/Teaching Collaborative between Wheelock College and the Brookline Public Schools has been in existence since the 1980s. Like other Professional Development Schools, its stated purpose is the improvement of the preservice education of teachers and the enhancement of teaching. This collaborative was among the first to reinforce the ideas of teachers as "boundary spanners," that is, teachers assume a variety of roles that usually are reserved either for grades K-12 or for higher education. For example, many teachers in the collaborative have become leaders in formulating classroom-based action research and have participated in the development of the statewide language arts curriculum framework, as well as developed new curricula. They have worked at the college level by presenting staff development workshops to both school and college faculty members. One of the collaborative's most consistent tenets has been that all teachers must assume a leadership role and be active in the collaborative's governance, making decisions about everything from budget to personnel.

The collaborative also introduced the concept of "Alternative Professional Time" (APT). In APT, year-long teaching interns assume responsibility for a classroom one day a week while regular teachers undertake research, improve courses, work in teams to restructure curriculum and improve school programs, and engage in college teaching and other endeavors that promote improved teaching.

Chief among the findings from evaluations of the collaborative is that teaching practices have changed significantly and involve more active learning. Also, the partnership has been found to be fragile, due to uncertainties about sustainable funding (Boles and Troen, 1997).

Informal Partnerships

Not all teacher education reform is occurring through PDS models. This section briefly describes several other approaches to the preparation of teachers that contain elements of reform (such as those suggested in Raizen and Michelsohn, 1994). These elements include approaching teacher education more coherently through collaboration with school districts across grades (K-12), encouraging clinical experience collaboration among science, education, and school faculty, and creating smoother transitions for new teachers from their university experiences to first-time employment.

Colorado College (Colorado Springs, Colorado)

Colorado College has long held that students' depth of knowledge in the liberal arts is a significant part of teacher education and needs to be balanced with an equally strong emphasis on clinical preparation. In order to accomplish these two goals, the college has established several fifth-year Master of Arts in Teaching (MAT) degree programs that lead to initial licensure in K-6 teaching and in secondary science or mathematics teaching. The fifth year design allows the college to recruit well-qualified candidates from a national pool of prospective teachers who have depth of content knowledge as well as initial experience in K-12 classrooms.

Using a 15-month design, elementary MAT candidates take education courses and engage in working with children their first summer, while secondary candidates take additional subject matter courses in science or mathematics. Both programs work with several local schools to identify appropriate placements that begin with the school year in late August for each cohort. In the first two months, candidates work half days as teachers' aides at the school while completing two educational methods courses. They then complete 8-10 weeks of full-time student teaching. A full-time internship follows in the second semester, contingent upon demonstrated performance during student teaching and receipt from the state of a Letter of Authorization, which permits these candidates to teach on their own with limited supervision. Additional coursework in education is taken during the second summer, completing the candidate's program.

Since 1997, faculty in the secondary science MAT program have used funds from the MacArthur Foundation (through the American Association for the Advancement of Science) to implement changes that link methods coursework, the student teaching/internship, and the induction period of a candidate's first year of teaching in local schools. Additional information about this program is available at <http://www.coloradocollege.edu/education>.

Georgia Southern University (Statesboro, Georgia)

Georgia Southern University's middle grades science program is based extensively on team teaching and collaboration. The science methods course is team-taught by faculty in both the College of Education and the College of Science and Technology. In addition, the students in this course are blocked together in a mathematics methods course. Activities and field trips are planned and shared by both courses and all instructors, providing a strong integration of content and pedagogy in both science and mathematics.

Purdue University (West Lafayette, Indiana)

Purdue University recently has revised its elementary teacher preparation program using a block schedule design (rather than a design where students take course independently of one another) and field placements in a selected "host school." Students are in the field for six semesters, beginning in their sophomore year and extending through student teaching. Students in cohort groups take "blocks" of courses each semester while engaging in field experience at the host school. A team consisting of K-5 teacher liaisons from the schools, Purdue education faculty, and graduate students in education teaches the courses. The content of the program is guided by INTASC guidelines and emphasizes diversity training, application of technology, and the use of student portfolios. Additional information about this program is available at <http://www.soe.purdue.edu/volkmann/edci205/TiP.html>.

Syracuse University (Syracuse, New York)

Syracuse University employs a "cycle of excellence" model for preparing secondary science teachers. The "professional core" of this program is a three-semester sequence of coursework, numerous field experiences, and student teaching placements. One goal is to provide a set of integrated and coherent experiences that will continually strengthen the candidates' professional development as science teachers. Each stage (semester) affords candidates opportunities to consider their current conception of effective science teaching and learning and to reflect on their growth and change as their ideas develop over time.

Candidates initially complete an entrance portfolio, in which they detail their emerging philosophy of teaching. When they take science methods during the second semester, candidates formalize their ideas about teaching and the decisions they will make in the classroom based on "best practices." This includes writing an extensive research-based rationale for how they will teach science. In the final stage of the cycle, candidates then explore an element of their paper through collaborative action research with their host teacher during their semester of student teaching. Their action research frequently causes them to revise their rationale for teaching science, to implement new teaching strategies, and to change their teaching portfolios.

University of Arizona (Tucson, Arizona)

The University of Arizona has designed a program, initially funded through the U.S. Department of Education's Eisenhower program, that specifically bridges the gap between teacher preparation and the first few years of teaching. The program supports beginning teachers in meeting once a month on Saturdays and also visits by a university science educator and teaching assistants five to six times the first year. School districts also support released time so that beginning teachers can observe each other's teaching and participate in local science education conferences.

The university also has created a combined Master's in Science Education and certification program with several unique features, including a yearlong student teaching experience, where candidates teach two classes each day. Half of the year is spent at the middle-school level and half at the high-school level. Practicum experience precedes this year of student teaching, and four core courses supplement and build upon the field experience: science methods, advanced science methods, history and philosophy of science, and how children learn science. The non-methods courses also enroll graduate teachers, allowing future teachers to work with experienced teachers on projects and course content. Candidates complete an exit project to demonstrate new knowledge in science education.

The University of Wisconsin-Milwaukee has reformed its middle/secondary science teacher education program and has doubled the number of students to 35 per year, adding many post-baccalaureate candidates with prior experience in business and industry. Prior to reform, the program offered a number of traditional courses, but they were not part of a holistic program. Rather they were disparate, stand-alone entities, lacking articulation with other courses in the program. Over time, this caused gaps and redundancies in the candidate's program. Today, highly coordinated courses and field experiences are delivered through a cohort of instructors as a result of the joint efforts of practicing teachers, education faculty, science faculty, and former students. The modified program now occupies three major blocks, with each block containing a core of field experience occurring at the middle- and high-school levels. There are reflective seminars and field experiences that are closely joined with coursework and with greater involvement by practicing teachers. A technology component is included. The program also has checkpoints and accountability.

Other Informal Partnerships: NSF's Collaboratives for Excellence in Teacher Preparation (CETP)[4]

In the early 1990s, the National Science Foundation established the Collaboratives for Excellence in Teacher Preparation (CETP) program to encourage active reform of teacher preparation programs. The goals of CETP include increasing the numbers of K-12 teachers who are well prepared in science, mathematics, and technology and encouraging faculty from the arts, sciences, engineering, and education to work together on improving science and mathematics teacher preparation. The collaboratives seek to broaden the pool of students who are interested in pursuing careers in teaching, including those majoring in science, mathematics, engineering, and technology and those traditionally underrepresented in those fields. A feature of most collaboratives is the integral involvement of two-year community colleges as partners with four-year institutions and K-12 school districts. CETP also seeks to improve undergraduate teaching and learning and to link undergraduate preparation of teachers to national standards in science and mathematics. In addition, the CETP program recognizes the importance of retaining new teachers, mentoring of new teachers by master teachers, and providing all teachers of science, mathematics, and technology with opportunities for continuing professional development and growth.

Each CETP-based program represents a unique effort to improve the quality of teacher education in science and mathematics. It has been observed that the uniqueness of each collaborative allows each one to serve as a model that potentially could be scaled up to a much larger level (Boyer and Layman, 1998). There is a great deal to be learned from the characteristics and lessons of these collaboratives, both individually and collectively. Examples of programs that have some degree of CETP funding are provided below.

Green River Community College (Auburn, Washington)[5]

Green River Community College has initiated **Project TEACH** (**T**eacher **E**ducation **A**lliance of **C**olleges and **H**igh Schools), a teacher preparation collaborative that demonstrates the role that community colleges can play in teacher preparation. The project in-

---

[4]Descriptions of the individual CETP programs can be accessed at <http://www.nsf.gov/cgi-bin/getpub?nsf9996>.

[5]Additional information about this program is available at <http://www.projectteach.org>.

cludes recruitment and preparation programs in six local school districts and Central Washington University. A significant goal of Project TEACH is to strengthen science and mathematics education in elementary schools through new interdisciplinary, standards-based courses for future teachers that model interactive teaching and active learning. Together, the community college and the university faculty have designed a new *Pre-Professional Associate of Arts Degree in Elementary Education* that builds a strong foundation for the university's certification program. The new two-year degree has the following components:

(1) a strong liberal arts foundation;

(2) introductory teacher education courses with embedded field-based assignments in diverse settings;

(3) a three-quarter mathematics sequence specifically designed for elementary teachers (number theory, geometry, and probability/statistics) that includes embedded field-based assignments with mentor elementary teachers; and

(4) a newly designed, three-quarter interdisciplinary and thematically-based science sequence that blends physics, geology, chemistry, and biology.

Other components of Project TEACH include (1) teacher clubs and recruitment activities in area high schools and at the community college; (2) tutoring at area schools and at a new, on-campus mathematics summer camp for fourth and fifth graders; (3) alternative pathways for teacher assistants and paraeducators; and (4) strong advising links and articulation with the teacher preparation program at the university.

Project TEACH is funded by a grant from the NSF through the CETP initiative and by the Washington State Office of Public Instruction, the Green River College Foundation, and individual contributors.

Henry Ford Community College (Dearborn, Michigan) [6]

Henry Ford Community College (HFCC) has designed Pre-Education Programs that articulate to teacher preparation programs at four-year institutions in the state. Motivated by the challenges presented by the Michigan Statewide Systemic Initiative, the HFCC programs are designed to (1) recruit students from under-represented groups, (2) provide mathematics courses that implement the NCTM Standards and the Michigan

---

[6]Additional information about this program is available at <http://www.hfcc.net/catalog/ programs_de.htm#Education>.

Curriculum Frameworks, (3) provide programs that articulate to teacher training institutions, and (4) incorporate early field experiences for all students. In addition, special initiatives developed by HFCC in conjunction with the University of Michigan-Dearborn, Eastern Michigan University, and Schoolcraft College (and made possible by NSF and Eisenhower Grant funds) have resulted in the development of Mathematics for Elementary Teachers courses implementing the Triesman model as well as mentorship activities with teachers from urban districts, and university/community college team field experiences in urban and bilingual classrooms. These projects have strengthened the community college students' experiences and provided a bridge from the community college to the university environments. Communities of mathematics educators and students from school districts, universities, and community colleges have formed. The success of the Pre-Education Programs at HFCC is partially documented by the programs' dramatic increase in pre-education declared majors, from 354 students in 1994 to 1,054 in 1998, with a proportionate increase in students designating minority status.

Summarizing the success of the mathematics curriculum, one African American student stated, "I can honestly say that I enjoy math now, and I am looking forward to teaching it. I hope to be able to inspire someone else.... Thank you so very much!"

Cerritos College (Norwalk, California)[7]

Cerritos College recently began a partnership with California State University, Long Beach (CSULB), to launch the Cerritos College Teacher TRaining ACademy (Teacher TRAC). Teacher TRAC gives future K-8 teachers an opportunity to complete their bachelor's degree and multi-subject teaching credential in four calendar years. Educational technology courses that help to enhance a K-8 teacher's ability and technology-proficiency in the classroom are a special feature of Teacher TRAC. Cerritos College faculty members are partnering with CSULB faculty to ensure that national, state, and local standards as well as technology are infused in core content courses. In addition, pedagogical practices are being rethought in light of inquiry-based, hands-on instructional practices. Cerritos College recently received grant funds from the California Chancellor's Office for a significant expansion of

---

[7]Additional information about this program is available at <http://www.teachertrac.org>.

Teacher TRAC. Funds will be used to address the critical need for recruitment of high school and community college students into educational programs leading to K-8 teaching careers. The grant also focuses on student development, faculty development, curriculum design, and fieldwork experiences for students. Cerritos College also is a partner with CSULB in an NSF CETP grant and a U.S. Department of Education technology grant.

Virginia Community College System (Richmond, Virginia)[8]

Virginia's community college system has launched a system-wide Teacher Preparation Initiative involving a faculty-in-residence position and a statewide Task Force with representatives from each of the Virginia higher education system's 23 community colleges. The goal of the initiative is to create new pathways for students in the community college system who want to become teachers. A statewide colloquium for arts and sciences and college of education representatives from two- and four-year institutions produced policy recommendations for the community college system in the areas of recruitment, collaboration, curriculum and advising, articulation with four-year institutions, early field experiences, and Praxis I preparation. Next steps include focusing on implementation of the policy recommendations and replicating programs that have been successful in targeting and supporting prospective teachers enrolled in the state's community colleges. Programs already identified as successful include specially designed orientation and career development courses, a teacher apprentice program, a baccalaureate transition program, and activities that stem from participation in the NSF-funded Virginia Collaborative for Excellence in the Preparation of Teachers (VCEPT).

---

[8]Additional information about this program is available at <http://www.so.cc.va.us/vccsasr/teacher.pdf>.

Appendix F
Biographical Sketches of
Committee Members

Herbert K. Brunkhorst (Co-chair) is professor of Science Education and Biology at California State University-San Bernardino, and chair of the Department of Science, Mathematics, and Technology Education in the College of Education. He carries a joint appointment in the Department of Biology in the College of Natural Sciences. Dr. Brunkhorst earned a Ph.D. with majors in science education and plant physiology at The University of Iowa. He has been a science educator for the past 33 years; 17 years at the precollege level and 16 at the college level. Dr. Brunkhorst was co-principal investigator of the National Science Foundation (NSF)-funded California State University Science Teaching Development Project from 1993-1995, a university system-wide collaboration to improve science teacher preparation. From 1995-1997, he served as a senior faculty researcher on a U.S. Department of

Education and Office of Educational Research and Improvement project called the Salish Consortium, a multidimensional collaborative research effort for improving science and mathematics teacher education. In 1998, Dr. Brunkhorst was selected as a California State University Chancellor's Teacher Preparation Scholar to serve as a member of a statewide teacher preparation curriculum development team to produce an Internet-based elementary teacher preparation program. For the past 11 years, Dr. Brunkhorst has served as co-director of the Inland Area Science Project, a regional collaborative professional development program in science for K-12 teachers under the sponsorship of the California Subject Matter Projects.

W. J. (Jim) Lewis (Co-chair) is chair of the Department of Mathematics and Statistics at the University of Nebraska-

Lincoln, where he has been a member of the faculty since 1971. Dr. Lewis holds B.S. and Ph.D. degrees in mathematics from Louisiana State University. His leadership in mathematics education includes a number of local, state, and national activities aimed at improving K-12 education and teacher preparation. He currently serves as chair of the Mathematical Association of America's Steering Committee on the Mathematics Education of Teachers. Dr. Lewis was co-principal investigator of the Nebraska National Science Foundation State Systemic Initiative from 1991-1997, and he regularly gives invited talks about education to new mathematics department chairs and new mathematics faculty members (via Project NeXT).

Toby Caplin has been a teacher since 1973. In 1974, she joined the Graham and Parks School, which is a racially, ethnically, economically diverse K-8 alternative public school in Cambridge, Massachusetts. In addition to teaching, Ms. Caplin is a staff developer for the Cambridge Public Schools mathematics department, for which she runs numerous inservice workshops on learning and teaching in mathematics. She also served as an educational consultant, primarily with Bolt Baranek and Newman in Cambridge, where she was the education specialist. The National Science Foundation (NSF)-funded

projects she has worked on include sense-making in science and inquiry in mathematics (involving videotape and other technologies). Ms. Caplin works in many capacities for her school's professional development relationship with the University of Massachusetts-Boston; she serves as a graduate seminar developer and co-teacher for practicum students and was the liaison between the two institutions for many years.

Rodney L. Custer has chaired the Department of Industrial Technology at Illinois State University in Normal, Illinois, since joining the faculty there in 1997. Dr. Custer earned a Ph.D. in Industrial Education at the University of Missouri-Columbia then joined the faculty there in 1991 as Assistant Professor in the Department of Practical Arts and Vocational-Technical Education. He is a national leader in technology education, and he chaired the secondary level standards development team for the Technology for All Americans project. He has been a member of the review board for the *Journal of Industrial Teacher Education*.

Penny J. Gilmer is professor of Chemistry at Florida State University, where she has been a member of the faculty since 1977. She holds a Ph.D. in Biochemistry from the University of California-Berkeley and is currently working toward a second doctorate, D.Sc.Ed., at Curtin University, Perth, Australia. In addition to holding faculty positions, she has served as associate department chair and interim associate dean of the College of Arts and Sciences. Dr. Gilmer has received funding from the National Science Foundation (NSF) for science teacher preparation and enhancement programs, which she has co-directed with colleagues in the College of Education. Her publications on science teacher preparation and professional development include action research investigations with preservice and inservice teachers. Her awards and distinctions include election as a fellow of the American Association for the Advancement of Science (AAAS) and the Innovation in Teaching Science Teachers award from the Association for the Education of Teachers of Science (AETS).

Martin L. Johnson is professor of Mathematics Education at the University of Maryland. He began his career as a junior and senior high-school mathematics and science teacher, then went on to receive the M.Ed. and Ed.D. degrees. He joined the faculty at the University of Maryland in 1972 and was promoted to full professor in 1986. He is currently chair of the Department of Curriculum and Instruction, a large

teacher education department charged with preparing elementary, secondary, college, and university teachers in a variety of content areas, including science and mathematics education. His work in mathematics education includes numerous peer-reviewed publications, leadership roles in mathematics education and minority educational organizations, and consulting positions with both K-12 and postsecondary education institutions. He has served as Senior Researcher for two National Science Foundation (NSF)-sponsored projects in mathematics education. In addition to his scholarship, Dr. Johnson has supervised more than 15 doctoral dissertations in mathematics education during his career at the University of Maryland.

Harvey B. Keynes is a professor of Mathematics, past director of education in the Geometry Center, and director of education programs for a new Institute of Technology Center at the University of Minnesota. His research interests are in dynamical systems. Professor Keynes has directed the following projects: The University of Minnesota Talented Youth Program; the National Science Foundation (NSF) Teacher Renewal Project; the NSF-supported Minnesota Mathematics Mobilization project; the Ford Foundation Urban Mathematics Collaborative; the NSF-supported Young Scholars Project; the

Bush Foundation Project to increase female participation in the University of Minnesota's Talented Youth Program; the NSF-funded Early Alert Initiative; and a new, reformed calculus program for engineering students. Professor Keynes also has taught calculus in the University of Minnesota's Talented Youth Program and has been a teacher in the NSF Teacher Renewal Project. He has extensive contacts in Minnesota and national mathematics education and high technology committees. He was a member of the National Research Council's Mathematical Sciences Education Board (MSEB) and is the recipient of the American Mathematical Society's 1992 Award for Distinguished Public Service.

R. Heather Macdonald is associate professor of Geology and chair of the Department of Geology at the College of William and Mary, where she recently served as dean of Undergraduate Studies, Arts and Sciences. She is a past president of the National Association of Geoscience Teachers (NAGT) and has co-organized numerous NAGT workshops on innovative and effective teaching and course design in the geosciences, as well as workshops for early career faculty. She also has served as chair of the Education Committee of the Geological Society of America and of the K-12 Earth Science

Education Committee of the Society for Sedimentary Geology (SEPM). She received the Biggs Earth Science Teaching Award from the Geological Society of America and the Thomas Jefferson Teaching Award from the College of William and Mary. Dr. Macdonald received a B.A. in geology from Carleton College and her M.S. and Ph.D. degrees in geology from the University of Wisconsin, Madison.

Mark Saul is a teacher at Bronxville High School, New York. He has taught high school for 28 years and has been an adjunct associate professor of Mathematics at City College of New York for 9 years. He also is director of the American Regions Mathematics League Russian Exchange Program. He received his Ph.D. in Mathematics Education from New York University in 1987. In 1981, he received the Sigma Xi Recognition for Outstanding High-School Science Teacher, Lehman College Chapter, and, for 1980-83, a Westinghouse Science Talent Search Certificate of Honor. In 1984, he received the Presidential Award for Excellence in the Teaching of Mathematics, National Science Foundation. In 1985, he received the Admiral Hyman L. Rickover Foundation Fellowship, was a Tandy Scholar in 1994, and received the Gabriella and Paul Rosenbaum Foundation Fellowship in 1995. Dr. Saul is a member of the Mathematical Sciences Education Board (MSEB) of the National Research Council (NRC) and is a fellow of the American Association for the Advancement of Science (AAAS). He has extensive experience as a judge of mathematical competitions and is an expert on Russian mathematics education. He is a member of the American Mathematical Society (AMS) and is active in the mathematics teaching standards revision effort of the National Council of Teachers of Mathematics (NCTM), currently chairing the Student Services Committee. Dr. Saul has been continuously active in professional workshops and presentations throughout his career and has authored over 20 publications.

M. Gail Shroyer is associate professor of Science Education at Kansas State University (KSU). She holds a B.A. in Biology from University of California - Santa Cruz and the M.S. and Ph.D. degrees in Curriculum and Instruction from KSU. She has an extensive background in science teacher preparation, including as coordinator of Professional Development Schools at KSU, as co-editor of the *Journal of Science Teacher Education*, and as principal investigator or director of numerous teacher education improvement projects supported by the U.S. Department of Education and the National Science Foundation. She

also has served as a member of the Advisory Board of the Association for the Education of Teachers in Science (AETS).

Larry Sowder is professor of Mathematics at San Diego State University. He received the B.S. and M.A.T. degrees from Indiana University, and then taught high-school mathematics and physics. After completing his Ph.D. in mathematics education at the University of Wisconsin, he joined the faculty at Northern Illinois University and was promoted to full professor in 1984. He moved to San Diego State University in 1986, where he continues to devote much of his attention to developing mathematics courses for preservice and inservice elementary and secondary mathematics teachers.

Dan B. Walker is professor of Biology and Science Education at San Jose State University. Dr. Walker is currently co-principal investigator of the San Francisco Bay Area Collaborative for Excellence in Teacher Preparation. He has won awards for teaching from both the University of Georgia and the University of California at Los Angeles. Dr. Walker developed an off-campus program for the employees of Lawrence Livermore Laboratory to obtain a Single Subject Teaching Credential in Science in California and is currently co-director of this program. He has published articles about this work, most recently in the form of essays in a volume on preparing scientists and mathematicians to become teachers.

VivianLee Ward is director of the Access Excellence program (founded by Genentech, Inc.), director of CyberEducation at the National Health Museum, and a former high-school biology teacher. She has presented numerous papers on science teacher development at meetings of the National Science Teachers' Association (NSTA), the American Association for the Advancement of Science (AAAS), the National Association of Biology Teachers (NABT), the American Educational Research Association (AERA), and Sigma Xi. During her decade of participation in the Stanford Teacher Education Project, she supervised 13 student teachers and interns. Ms. Ward has consulted nationwide in relation to science education, professional development, and uses of technology in education. She has received many accolades for her teaching and other contributions to life science education, including the Labosky Award for Outstanding Contribution to Teacher Education (1989), the California Outstanding Biology Teacher Award (1992), and Mentor Teacher of the Year Award (1994). She is on the Advisory Boards of the California

Science Subject Matter Project and SETI's Voyage Through Time Project and is currently completing her doctorate in Teaching and Learning at the University of Southern California.

Lucy West is director of Mathematics, K-12, in New York City's Community School District 2. She is presently principal investigator for a National Science Foundation Local Systemic Change project on teacher enhancement that involves over 1,200 teachers in 48 schools. Ms. West is a District Fellow at the Learning Research and Development Center, University of Pittsburgh, where she is working on a research project that centers around the development of effective coaching strategies for practicing teachers: Content Focused Coaching. She is an adjunct instructor teaching mathematics methods courses at City College of New York and at Bank Street College of Education. Ms. West has consulted nationwide in relation to mathematics education and professional development. She is a member of the National Council of Supervisors of Mathematics (NCSM), the National Council of Teachers of Mathematics (NCTM), the Association for Supervision and Curriculum Development (ASCD), and the National Council of Staff Developers (NCSD).

Susan S. Wood is professor of Mathematics, J. Sargeant Reynolds Community College, Richmond, Virginia, and president of the American Mathematical Association of Two-Year Colleges (AMATYC). She was a member of the Mathematical Sciences Education Board (MSEB) of the National Research Council (NRC) from 1998-2000. She received her Ed.D. in Mathematics Education from the University of Virginia in 1979. She has taught mathematics at the community college level for the past 27 years. Her awards include the first J. Sargeant Reynolds Community College Sabbatical, 1996; Distinguished Service in Mathematics Education Award, 1995; William C. Lowry Outstanding Mathematics Teacher Award, Virginia Council of Teachers of Mathematics, 1995; Faculty Development Grant, 1995; Chancellors Commonwealth Professor, 1994; Employee Recognition, 1990 and 1994; State Council of Higher Education for Virginia Outstanding Faculty Award, 1992; and Outstanding Work in Developmental Studies, 1989. Dr. Wood has strong ties to several mathematics professional organizations, is significantly involved in mathematics education reform at the national level, and has made more than 100 conference presentations to students and teachers since 1990. She is a member of the Mathematical Association of America (MAA) and the National Council of Teachers of Mathematics (NCTM). For six years she served as the Mid-Atlantic Vice President of AMATYC.

Glossary of Education Terms

Like all other professionals, educators use language and terms that are specific to the profession. In fact, many people inside and outside of education claim that there can be no "profession" without a special language. This glossary is provided for readers who may not be familiar with some of the words and concepts commonly used by professional educators.

As with other professions, in education, the use and meaning of certain terms is constantly evolving. Indeed, a given term in education might be defined in more than one way, in part because so many different professional communities influence education. Therefore, this glossary points out many nuances but does not necessarily provide all the definitions or usages of a given term.

Term	Definition
Accreditation	The granting of approval by an official accrediting body for a college or university to conduct its programs at the undergraduate level. For preservice education, there are two primary organizations that provide such accreditation to colleges and universities: the National Council for Accreditation of Teacher Education (NCATE)[1] and the Teacher Education Accreditation Council (TEAC)[2].

---

[1]Additional information about NCATE is available at <http://www.ncate.org/>. Information about the recently released NCATE standards is available at http://www.ncate.org/2000/pressrelease.htm.
[2]Additional information about TEAC is available at <http://www.teac.org/>.

Conceptual Understanding	Assists in drawing distinctions between knowing how to do something (procedural or skill understanding) and knowing what something means (conceptual understanding). For example, understanding $1\frac{3}{4}$ divided by $\frac{1}{2}$ should include both how to do the calculation (procedural understanding) and what $1\frac{3}{4}$ divided by $\frac{1}{2}$ means (conceptual understanding); i.e., being able to calculate a derivative of a function is different from knowing what that derivative means.
Content Specialist	A person who has extensive training in and knowledge of a subject area and can both teach that subject to students and help other teachers become more knowledgeable about the subject. Most commonly, this term is used to describe teachers in grades K-12 who have focused their education on mastering the content of specific disciplines. In science and mathematics education, there has been an ongoing debate about whether content specialists are needed and appropriate to teach these subjects effectively in the primary and middle grades.
Endorsement	In a subject area—acknowledges that a teacher has studied that subject area at such a level and with enough demonstrated proficiency to be able to teach it effectively. Teachers may seek endorsements in more than one area of expertise that complements or expands understanding of their primary content area of knowledge. For example, in some states a teacher may be certified to teach in the secondary grades with an endorsement in science. In other cases, a teacher may be certified to teach science with an endorsement in physics.
Field Component of Teacher Education	The time that preservice teachers spend in schools and classrooms working with mentor teachers. The practicum is considered to be one part of a preservice teacher's field component of teacher education. Commonly, a faculty member from the student teacher's college or university oversees field components. Increasingly, field components of teacher

education may involve longer term, intensive, paid or unpaid internships. In some teacher education programs, field experiences also may begin well before the senior year or be scheduled during a fifth undergraduate year.

Induction Phase   Encompasses the first years of teaching after a student completes a preservice teacher education program (commonly the first one to three years of teaching). A great deal of research points to the induction phase or period as critical in a new teacher's decision to continue in or leave the profession.

Inquiry   Although used in different ways by different authors, most generally refers to the myriad ways in which scientists study nature and propose explanations for natural phenomena based on the evidence derived from their work. Inquiry also can refer to the abilities that students and teachers need to develop to be able to design and conduct scientific investigations. It also refers to the kinds of understandings they develop about the nature of science and how scientific investigation is undertaken. "Inquiry" also can refer to approaches and strategies for teaching and learning that enable learners to master scientific concepts as a result of carrying out scientific investigations.

For further information about the nature and role of inquiry in teaching and learning, see National Research Council (2000b).

Inservice Education   The professional development programs that are offered to practicing classroom teachers. There is little agreement about what should constitute inservice education. Programs range from workshops held as part of teacher professional development days during the school year to formal courses offered by peers or at colleges and universities.

Lower Division Course   A course offered by a college or university that typically would be taken by first or second year undergraduate students.

Usually, lower division courses fulfill a college- or university-wide requirement (such as a distribution or general education requirement) for graduation.

Master/Mentor Teacher

A teacher with extensive levels of teaching experience and demonstrated effectiveness in the classroom who may provide mentoring and professional guidance to less experienced colleagues in a variety of ways. Currently, few guidelines exist for determining which teachers qualify as master or mentor teachers. Increasingly, master teachers are being called upon to work with their colleagues in colleges and universities to improve teaching practice or the content of specific courses or curricula. For example, master teachers may team-teach courses for preservice teachers or may offer a variety of professional development activities for more experienced teachers.

Out-of-Field Teaching

Teachers teaching subject areas in which they do not have endorsement and in which they have little or no formal training. Although the definition is not precise, out-of-field teaching often refers to teaching in subject areas in which the teacher did not earn a major or minor during the undergraduate years and in which he or she does not have an endorsement.

PDS

Professional Development School (see Chapter 5 for a more complete description). Also see definition below.

Pedagogical Content Knowledge

Shulman (1986) was the first to propose the concept of pedagogical content knowledge, stating that it "...embodies the aspects of content most germane to its teachability ... pedagogical content knowledge includes for the most regularly taught topics in one's subject area, the most useful forms of representation of those ideas, the most powerful analogies, illustrations, examples, explanations, and demonstrations—in a word, the ways of representing and formulating the subject that makes it comprehensible to others.... [It] also includes an understanding of what makes the learning of specific concepts easy or difficult: the conceptions and preconceptions that students of different ages and backgrounds bring with them to the learning."

Thus, pedagogical content knowledge is a type of knowledge that may be unique to teaching. It is based on the ways that teachers relate what they know about what they teach (subject matter knowledge) to what they know about effective teaching (pedagogical knowledge). The synthesis and integration of these two types of knowledge characterize *pedagogical content knowledge* (Cochran, 1997).

Different disciplines may require a variety of approaches to teaching in order for students to learn the content of that discipline effectively. *Pedagogical content knowledge* implies that teachers know the content of the discipline and that they teach, organize, and represent that content in ways that address students' needs and enhance learning.

Practicum   Usually refers to the time toward the end of the preservice education experience that student teachers are able to work with teachers and engage in actual classroom teaching as well as a variety of related experiences. In some cases, practicum refers to "student teaching." However, it also may refer to shorter periods of time when students, especially those who are beginning in teacher education, can gain experience in schools to help them decide whether they would like to continue pursuing teaching as a career.

Praxis   A series of examinations administered by the Educational Testing Service that are used to assess qualifications both for admission into teacher education programs at some colleges and universities and for certification following the completion of a preservice program. Thirty-five of the 43 states that now require an examination for new teachers use the Praxis series. Additional information about this examination is available at <http://www.teachingandlearning.org/licnsure/praxis/prxfaq.html>.

Preservice Education

The programs at institutions of higher education (typically through schools or colleges of education) that prepare new teachers for grades K-12.

Professional Community

The community that is responsible for preparing, providing professional development for, and supporting teachers throughout their careers. Recent efforts to improve teacher education and professionalism have involved engaging members of the K-12, higher education, and business and industry communities.

Professional Development School

A formal collaboration between a college or university and the K-12 sector for the specific purpose of improving teacher education and school renewal.

Reflective Practice (Practitioner)

"... a mode that integrates or links thought and action with reflection. It [reflective practice] involves thinking about and critically analyzing one's actions with the goal of improving one's professional practice. Engaging in reflective practice requires individuals to assume the perspective of an external observer in order to identify the assumptions and feelings underlying their practice and then to speculate about how these assumptions and feelings affect practice" (Imel, 1992).

School Practitioner

Anyone who engages in the act of teaching. Most often the term refers to teachers of grades K-12, but it also is occasionally used to refer to those who instruct in higher education.

Teacher Education

Used to describe either preservice or inservice education but also sometimes used to describe the continuum of teacher preparation and professional development. As emphasized in this report, teacher education is a concept that would supplant the separation of various phases of a teacher's professional life (preservice education, induction, and inservice education or professional development). The concept of teacher education would weave these phases into a much more seamless and integrated continuum of education that helps all teachers grow and develop professionally.

Teacher Educator   Traditionally, faculty in schools and colleges of education who prepare new teachers, provide professional development for practicing teachers, and conduct research on the improvement of education and teaching. However, this report calls for a broadening of the concept of teacher educator to include all educators who are involved with teacher education. For teachers of science, mathematics, and technology, this would include faculty in the life and physical sciences, mathematics, and engineering. It also would include master teachers who work in any capacity with faculty in higher education to provide high-quality teacher education programs.

Teacher Intern   Someone who undertakes one of several different kinds of learning opportunities for prospective or practicing teachers. In some cases, practicing teachers intern formally in business, industry, or a research laboratory to learn more about the needs of the workplace and how their teaching might better prepare students for these kinds of challenges and opportunities. In some cases, teacher interns are prospective teachers who through their internships can pursue much longer and more intense teaching experiences than might be available in a practicum or other field experience. Interns are often provided with stipends—an increasingly important practice for those who are considering teaching as a career but who also have family and other obligations that require them to earn income before becoming employed as teachers.

Teacher Licensing and Certification
The granting of official recognition, usually by a state's department of education, that an individual teacher is qualified to teach at one or more grade levels or in one or more subject areas. In some states, new teachers may receive provisional certification until they have completed additional study or have demonstrated in some way their ability to teach at a given grade level in a given subject area.

Teaching Practice
The art of teaching that involves employing content knowledge and pedagogy that is appropriate for a given subject area and for the developmental level of the students being taught, as well using one's knowledge of students' abilities and learning styles. Teaching practice is influenced by a host of factors such as a teacher's own educational background and experiences, his or her knowledge and use of the research literature on teaching, and the condition of the school and community where teaching and learning are taking place.

Teaching as Telling or Teaching Is Telling
A phrase sometimes used by educators to describe an approach to teaching that is characterized by excessively formal presentation. Often this kind of teaching involves little or no solicitation of student input. Explicit connections are not made to students' prior or related knowledge. The learning that results and is measured may emphasize memorization more than conceptual development.

Index

U

V

W